CO-CREATION AND SMART CITIES

CO-CREATION AND SMART CITIES: LOOKING BEYOND TECHNOLOGY

BY

SHENJA VAN DER GRAAF

University of Twente, The Netherlands

LE ANH NGUYEN LONG

University of Twente, The Netherlands

AND

CARINA VEECKMAN

imec-SMIT, Vrije Universiteit Brussel, Belgium

United Kingdom – North America – Japan – India
Malaysia – China

Emerald Publishing Limited
Howard House, Wagon Lane, Bingley BD16 1WA, UK

First edition 2022

Reprints and permissions service
Contact: permissions@emeraldinsight.com

British Library Cataloguing in Publication Data
A catalogue record for this book is available from the British Library

ISBN: 978-1-80043-603-9 (Print)
ISBN: 978-1-80043-602-2 (Online)
ISBN: 978-1-80043-604-6 (Epub)

Printed and bound by CPI Group (UK) Ltd, Croydon, CR0 4YY

ISOQAR certified Management System, awarded to Emerald for adherence to Environmental standard ISO 14001:2004.

ISOQAR
REGISTERED
Certificate Number 1985
ISO 14001

INVESTOR IN PEOPLE

CONTENTS

LIST OF FIGURES

ABOUT THE AUTHORS

Shenja van der Graaf, PhD, is an Assistant Professor of Communication Science at the University of Twente (UT) in The Netherlands. Her interests focus on digital transformations and the cultural, economic and governance dynamics that accompany them, such as for firms, cities and user communities. She has held research, advisory and management positions at public and private entities in Belgium, UK, Japan, and USA, and authored various articles and books. Before joining the UT, she was a Principle Investigator at imec-SMIT, Vrije Universiteit Brussel (VUB), leading the 'Data, Governance & Communities' Unit.

Le Anh Nguyen Long, PhD, is an Assistant Professor of Public Administration at the UT in The Netherlands. Her teaching and research focus on how local governments, in their capacity as laboratories of democracy, can contribute new and needed solutions through their policy experiments and innovations. She is an Executive Board Member of the European Urban Research Association and a Research Fellow at the Center for Environmental Policy and Behavior at the University of California (UC), Davis.

Carina Veeckman is a Senior Researcher and Project Manager at imec-SMIT, VUB, in Belgium. Her interests focus on participatory governance and citizen science, as well as social innovation through collaborative platforms. She is a part of the 'Data, Governance & Communities' Unit at SMIT and serves as the Principle Investigator on citizen science with two recent science communication handbooks. She is a Board Member of Scivil, the Knowledge Centre for Citizen Science in Flanders.

ACKNOWLEDGEMENTS

The idea for this book is a 'derivative' outcome of a co-creation workshop organised by the Data, Governance & Communities (previously, Smart Cities) Unit during the 2018 Strategic Days of Studies in Media, Innovation and Technology (imec-SMIT, Vrije Universiteit Brussel). The focus at that time was on listing and developing co-creation methods and tools that were being, or should be used, in many of our city-related research projects. Over time, this ambition shifted towards offering a critical, thorough, yet practical introduction on how to facilitate and optimise citizen involvement by implementing and deploying co-creation methods within cities, thereby putting public value at the centre of future development in the increasingly complex, multi-stakeholder ecosystem of urban public and private entities.

We would like to explicitly thank Jonas Breuer, Francesca Spagnoli, Laura Temmerman and Mehdi Montakhabi for their contributions. Jonas, your view on co-creation helped to design the flowchart and to keep the privacy and ethical aspects of co-creation in view. Francesca, your input and link with Living Labs helped to frame the design principles on co-creation as well as the various methods and tools for the co-creation flowchart. Laura, your practical insights helped to further streamline the co-creation flowchart and helped to finalise its last puzzles. Finally, Mehdi, thank you for your help with layouting, referencing, and being supportive throughout the process. This book would not have been possible without your contributions.

We are grateful for the many lively discussions, intellectual stimulation, puzzled looks, and 'interrogations' we got from our colleagues ('Smitters') during Unit and other meetings and the occasional water cooler or hallway conversation. In particular, a big thank you to Nils Walravens, Bram Lievens, Olga Tsoumani, Jaco van der Bank, Koen Borghys, Ruben D'Hauwers, Ine van Zeeland, Annelien Smets, Rob Heyman, Ilse Mariën, Simon Delaere, Jo Pierson and, last but not least, Pieter Ballon.

A very special thank you to Wim Vanobberghen. You are Epic and you know it.

Also, we would like to express our words of gratitude to 'a decade of colleagues', spread across Europe, UK, South Africa and USA, whom we collaborated with on numerous research projects, Living Labs, City of Things (Antwerp), and other settings.

A special thanks for all the interviewees who provided a testimonial and words of wisdom about their experiences with co-creation: Lieven Raes (Informatie Vlaanderen), Matteo Satta (Issy-les-Moulineaux), Rib Drabs (Luchtpijp), Martijn de Waal (The Amsterdam University of Applied Sciences), Paulo Calçada (Porto Digital) and Inese Viktorija Grospine (The Ministry of Environmental Protection and Regional Development of the Republic of Latvia).

Our colleagues at the University of Twente, especially, Alexander van Deursen, Sjoerd de Vries, and René Torenvlied, thank you for your warm welcome, guidance and support.

Thanks also to Francesco Catania for your ideas, and for being a much needed sounding board. And, to our (extended) families and friends, thanks for bearing with us.

Shenja, Le Anh, and Carina
July 2021

Chapter 1

INTRODUCTION

The city of Carouge (Switzerland) 'occasionally' engages in co-creation activities with citizens and other stakeholders – co-creation is viewed as a social network, meaning that if nobody participates, it is unlikely to survive.

The city of Eindhoven (The Netherlands) 'often' deploys co-creation to involve citizens, entrepreneurs, and organisations in developing policies and tailored projects, in particular. Co-creation is said to be a prerequisite for the well-accepted implementation and the functioning of the city's 'smart' services, especially those directed at improving the quality of life for its citizens.

The city of Helsinki (Finland) uses co-creation 'constantly', especially, to develop digital services and to open up data and application programming interfaces, as well as for urban planning activities.

Cities have different uses for and experiences with co-creation as is evidenced by these three illustrations[1] (Spagnoli, van der Graaf, & Brynskov, 2019). The concept of co-creation resonates with the increasingly citizen-centric discourse associated with the 'smart' city imaginary, a label which has been appropriated by many cities around the globe. While its exact meaning may not be easy distilled from relevant literatures that span various domains, such as media, urban and business studies, it seems to hold roots in, arguably, normative framings wherein technology plays primarily a facilitating role and signifies what it means for citizens to live in cities these days. Physical and digital boundaries of the city are said to have blurred facilitated by various technologies and infrastructures and, increasingly, shaped by information and communication technologies (ICTs) such as platforms and urban services pro-vided by companies like Google (e.g., Waze). While gradually implicated in shaping the structures of our everyday lives in the city, 'the unique affordances of platforms are said to signal an evolution of the socio-technical relationship between citizens and cities' (Lee, Mackenzie, Smith, & Box, 2020, p. 116), what has been termed 'platform urbanism' (Barns, 2020; van der Graaf & Ballon, 2019). Public and private organisations can tap value from this ever-more complex urban ecosystem, such as via emerging service models and tailored interventions (cf. Graham, Kitchin, Mattern, & Shaw, 2019; Parker, Van Alstyne, & Choudary, 2017). Moreover, as these ecosystems can record, quantify, and process enormous volumes of data derived from physical and digital spheres, all facets of our lives (e.g., our preferences, social relationships, and bodies) are being monitored and turned into datasets via everyday encounters and interactions with technologies like sensors and smartphones (cf. Lupton, 2018). While some welcome these developments, others point to the possible risks for citizens and society (Couldry & Yu, 2018; Zambonelli, Salim, Loke, De Meuter, & Kanhere, 2018).

Popular and academic debates have intensified on this dynamic associated with 'participation' and 'datafication', highlighting an apparent 'data fetishization' and the glossing over of human elements and agency in urban processes (van der Graaf, 2020). In today's desire to 'smarten up' emphasising citizens as integral to socio-technological processes – operationalised by the co-creation concept – that shape the urban environment, the investigation into the framing of citizen roles is warranted (cf. Kitchin, Cardullo, & Feliciantonio, 2019). The premise of co-creation for public administrations, such as cities, is to yield insights into how to better serve citizens by gathering information about their needs, preferences, patterns, and the like, guiding the creation and enhancement of sophisticated services, policies and other outcomes tailored to their needs. At present, most, if not all, smart city initiatives assert to be 'citizen-focused' or 'citizen-centric', which, arguably, may be more of a theoretical-normative instead of a materiality. Moreover, it seems to be challenged by an ongoing data-centred discourse that 'speaks' on behalf of citizens, as well as, in practice, some groups like children who are left behind (van der Graaf, 2020). It may, therefore, not come as a surprise that conceiving the role of citizens in the urban space has triggered a renewed interest in the 'right to the city' (Cardullo, Di Feliciantonio, & Kitchin, 2019; Lefebvre, 1968). The right to the city 'is not merely a right of access to what already exists, but a right to change it after our heart's desire' (Harvey, 2003, p. 939), underpinned by 'a new urban commons, a public sphere of active democratic participation' (p. 941) that is inclusive and collaborative.

This book seeks to contribute to the debate about the ever-increasing role of ICTs in cities and their inclusiveness of citizens, in specific. In fact, cities are possibly the most dynamic and important administrative units today. They have a significant role to play in many of the complex challenges the world is facing, such as climate change, aging and migration. This places pressure on public administrations, to do more with less, especially at the local level where public services tend to have the greatest impact on people's everyday lives. At the same time, governments and society more broadly, are experiencing a fundamental shift associated with the rise of so-called platform economies and new consumption patterns, transforming public service development and delivery. With these, also the compositions of public values (e.g., privacy, accountability, transparency) are altering. Not only do city administrations work hard to keep up with these changes but also with shifting expectations of citizens and – motivated by a 'responsible innovation' perspective – explore ways in which they can meet these requirements with a more robust value-based perspective of public service development and delivery (Cluley & Radnor, 2020; Stilgoe, Owen, & Macnaghten, 2013). Co-creation is considered a valid means to support the 'balancing act' for cities and other public service organisations of putting forward efficient and cost-effective governance supported by endless 'smart' and 'collaborative innovation' solutions, as well as developing a citizen-centric focus that is sustainable (or, long-lasting) over time.

At present, a holistic approach is lacking for systematically achieving an equilibrium between the diverse interests that make up the multi-stakeholder and multi-sector setting of a city. In complex, diverse urban environments assigning active, coequal and structural roles to all involved has not been achieved despite the wide range of available technologies and methods, particularly, those associated with 'smart' city ideals (Breuer, Walravens, van der Graaf, & Mariën, 2019). This introduction, therefore, sets the stage by drawing out the current dynamics that materialise between citizens and the smart city concept, followed by an outline of the structure of the book.

1.1. 'SMART' CITY IN CONTENTION? PARTICIPATION, DATAFICATION AND RIGHTS

The urban concept of 'smart city' is widespread. In the 1980s, it emerged to denote changes in the urban realm related to ICTs and urban systems innovations. It was only from the 2000s that the term caught on as a planning and development paradigm central to the operations and governance, of urban space and, in extension, seems to support the (altering) basic principles of what it means to live in cities whereby, arguably, public space is 'translated' into 'code', and 'code' can be seen to 'reshape' the urban space, or society more broadly (Kitchin & Dodge, 2011; Komninos & Mora, 2018). It should be noted, however, that to date, there is no agreement about nor is there a precise rationale and meaning of the smart city concept. Approaching it as a framework, a focus on pragmatic and functional aspects seems to come to the fore, accompanied by critiques (such as inclusion of vulnerable citizens, privacy) and ambitious solutionist-driven visions to tackle these gripping complexities (van der Graaf, 2020). Also, rather than being driven by a spatial vision, the smart city concept seems to hold more of a thematic orientation, such as citizen engagement, transportation, the environment, and public safety, thereby highlighting supporting axes of technology-driven and human-driven, top-down and bottom-up planning, as well as collective intelligence and data-driven intelligence in the smart city literature (cf. Hatuka, Rosen-Zvi, Birnhack, Toch, & Zur, 2018). Consequently, Breuer and Pierson (2021, p. 799) recently summed up:

> Despite the multifaceted debate around, and application of, the smart city concept [...] What can be studied are manifold, diverse, sometimes overlapping, often siloed projects. They are mostly data-driven as well as local in nature, they address diverse aspects of urban life and governance, promising local government efficiency on a reduced budget [...]. Many focus on technical aspects [...]. These are often proof-of-concepts and experiments that could, potentially, enable citywide innovations. What this data may enable or solve is, however, vague and its potential assumed.

With technology and ICTs being paramount in the 'smart' functioning of the urban space comes the capacity of producing, processing, and extracting value from various data streams like people, households and urban areas. Concepts such as 'datafication' and 'datafied cities' are useful for pointing to such data-driven correlations (e.g., behaviour-spatial tracking) – the practices that are used to make inferences about participations, affiliations, and predispositions, and which come hand in hand with all kinds of ethical issues, such as about privacy, social sorting and nudging. Not only do these materialities of data regimes demand critical attention, but also the practice of changing people into 'data assemblages', where instead of people speaking for themselves, the data are speaking for them (van der Graaf, 2020; cf. Livingstone, 2019). It is in this setting that citizen participation has, more recently, pushed to the top rank on the agenda of 'smart city'-making, indicative of a seeming 'human/e' turn (Almeida, Doneda, & da Costa, 2018; Oliveira & Campolargo, 2015). Far from being a new practice, the conceptualisation of the term participation is ambiguous, associated with diverse approaches and evaluations across domains (cf. Carpentier, 2016). In the smart city context, participation tends to be seen, or to occur, within the confines of a small-scale, local project and, hence, tends to impact or contribute to democratic processes in this capacity. Notwithstanding the diffusion of interest in participation, the smart city literature centre-stages the role of citizens, their communities and social capital in general in its technological innovation trajectory, thereby highlighting mantras like 'citizen-focus' and 'citizen-centric' in support of this vision (cf. de Waal & Dignum, 2017). In this way, city-making involves a multi-stakeholder approach to enhance the cities' capacity to learn, innovate and transform.

Consulting the literature on participation – adjacent to the discourse on 'citizenship' – and the degree to which citizens participate in urban life has shown, however, that they seem largely excluded (Mosco, 2019), put aptly by Kitchin, Cardullo, and Feliciantonio (2018, p. 11):

> [...] most often occupy non-participatory, consumer or tokenistic positions and are framed within political discourses of stewardship, technocracy, paternalism and the market, rather than being active, engaged participants where smart city initiatives are conceived in terms of rights, citizenship, the public good, and the urban commons. [...]. If there is civic engagement it is in the form of a participant, tester or player who provides feedback or suggestions, rather than being a proposer, co-creator, decision-maker or leader.

Furthermore, in the literature – alongside the stream of thought concerned with the 'datafied city' – citizens tend to be labelled not only as citizen but are also referred to by terms including 'user', 'data point' and 'surveilled subject', downplaying the role citizens play, or rather, making it perhaps implicit. This resonates with the so-called 'participation society' premise where public-sector reforms (motivated by cost savings, efficiency, and so forth) place greater responsibility on citizens while, simultaneously, asking citizens to contribute to governance endeavours more diligently (Buijs et al., 2019) – a marketisation of sorts the dynamics of which have brought questions about the social (in)justice of city living (Mitchell, 2003) back into play. And with this, a 'right's turn' including debates around data protection, sparked by a renewed interest in people's agency. In this environment where interest in different, interlocking rights is being mobilised, citizens and government play a crucial role in ensuring that rights are acknowledged and realised.

The concept of 'rights' is itself fuzzy and ill-defined. One of the main questions concerning rights is *who* possesses them. By participating, citizens make a claim on their 'right to the city', and when they engage with and reshape space, citizens exercise their right to appropriation (Lefebvre, Kofman, & Lebas, 1996; Purcell, 2002). Essentially, Lefebvre's notion of the Right to the City (Lefebvre, 1968) paints citizens as important actors who actively participate in decision-making processes that shape urban development (Kitchin et al., 2019; Purcell, 2002). Activity in the smart city centres as much on data as it does on citizens, who the new technologies and methods target for more intense participation in decision-making on urban development. Yet, as mentioned, this conceptualisation of citizenship rarely materialises in practice. The emphasis on rights, particularly in urban contexts, is reinvigorated by the increasing digitalisation of urban landscapes. More specifically, the debate around what constitutes the right to the city (Lefebvre, 1968) has been revitalised in light of the increasingly contested nature of information and personal data, how it is produced, used, owned, stored, and explained.

Thus, there is an overlap between the discourse on the rights to the city in an era where cities are trying to 'smarten' up and supranational mobilisation for the recognition of fundamental rights to privacy and data protection (Edwards, 2016; Loideain, 2019). These latter rights have become enshrined in the EU's General Data Protection Regulation (GDPR) of 2016. The right to be informed and to be forgotten are just two among the bundle of rights embodied by the GDPR. In this regard, Foth, Tomitsch, Satchell, and Hank Haeusler's (2015) articulation of the concepts of use, usage and usability provide a nuanced view on the relationship between citizens and technology, this view aligns with ideas and ideals that lie at the core of the continent's data protection policies like empowerment, self-determination, accountability and transparency (see also 'privacy impact assessment' in Breuer & Pierson, 2021). These ideas also align with the spirit embodied in the right to the city, which is also geared towards citizen empowerment albeit in a broader sphere.

There are also, however, important deviations between Europe's data regime and ideas encapsulated by 'the right to the city'. For instance, the GDPR places the individual at the centre with its focus on the right to privacy and the right to self-determination (Cohen, 2019). This stands in contrast to the emphasis on community empowerment within the discourse on the 'right to the city'. Neglecting community leads to the design and deployment of projects that reduces the citizen to a passive actor; the citizen-as-user is a subject of technical experiment and not an equal stakeholder of the value being co-created. Projects that leverage this view tend to emphasise corporate interests in, for example, trying to reckon with the introduction of GDPR and developing technologies while foregoing direct consultation with citizens as data-subjects (Breuer & Pierson, 2021). Thus, the smart city rhetoric can be critiqued for disguising inequality and to act as a 'boosting mechanism' in promoting the 'smart city' as a business model instead of benefitting social justice and is said to be deeply embedded in the neo-liberal ethos (Hatuka et al., 2018). Furthermore, the growing control of (local) governments over their citizens is called into question, such as in terms of data/surveillance and also the increasingly complex ('black box') public–private platform-based ecosystem (De Lange & De Waal, 2019).

In sum, the contradictions between collective benefits and rights, on the one hand, and the individualisation of responsibility and benefit, on the other, are increasingly becoming apparent (van der Graaf, 2020). These contradictions persist despite attempts to employ a range of participatory mechanisms (e.g., Living Labs, citizen science), because in the end, the mechanisms seem to work in favour of the projects themselves and less so the participants (Cardullo, Kitchin, & Di Feliciantonio, 2017). A citizen-centric view which neglects the networked nature of citizens, that is that their citizenship is primarily informed by their sense of belonging to a community, emphasises procedures and technologies and tries to find regulatory solutions to deep-seated societal problems like bias, fairness, accountability, and transparency (Kitchin, 2021; Townsend, 2013), possibly further stiffening those issues by supporting the social and institutional infrastructures that give rise to them (Cardullo et al., 2019). In light of the tendency to treat citizens as users rather than as equal stakeholders, the research community is increasingly interested in how different technologies, for example, platforms, shape the relationships that make up the socio-technical systems that we call 'smart cities'. This highlights the need for a shift in mindset whereby instead of seeing 'smartening' technologies as the main pathway to a better city, they are seen as a means of supporting a future city which emphasises values like fairness, tolerance, and wellbeing (Peña Gangadharan & Niklas, 2019). In this way, smart city technologies are reframed as part of a wider structure to address wicked problems like racism and inequality (cf. 'decentring smart cities' in Kitchin, 2021). Therefore, rather than an end goal, smartening up exists to reinforce social, economic, and environmental interventions in a context which while employing other means and methods also work towards equity, justice, and openness in the city (Morozov & Bria, 2018). Another strategy would be to more clearly delimit what we mean by public value in order to improve efforts to generate it (cf. O'Flynn, 2021). The premise of this book is that co-creation can be the point of departure that lies exactly at the intersection of relational and public value perspectives, which can be leveraged to achieve sustainable solutions that will be more just for all, benefitting our present and future communities, cities and society, at large.

1.2. OVERVIEW OF THE BOOK

The remainder of this book is divided into five chapters, which can be read consecutively from cover to cover, or each chapter can be read as a self-contained piece.

Chapter 2 – Co-creation has the potential to transform how we address deep-seated environmental, economic, and social problems, thereby allowing us to attain our aspirations for our cities and the communities housed within. In order to be meaningful, however, co-creation must consider mutual dependencies between all stakeholders, especially citizens. Chapter 2 does just that, by first reflecting on the concept of co-creation and considering it with respect to its relationship to similar concepts like co-production, co-design and user-driven innovation, recognising the different conceptual views in different disciplines. This discussion is then opened up with an interrogation into the possibilities for co-creation given the evolving relationship between citizens and the range of Public Service Organisations (PSOs) that make up city government. The chapter then launches into an exploration of the central challenges experienced by PSOs when embarking on a co-creation project and ends with a reflection on the approach's potentialities.

Chapter 3 – Design principles are necessary for overcoming the risks and challenges associated with co-creation. Here, *six guiding principles* ('6C Framework') *for concretely and effectively enacting co-creation with citizens* is presented. This framework can be used for assessing the current situation and reflecting on the aspirations of co-creators. Essentially, these guiding principles support the identification of a set of methods and tools (presented in more detail in Chapter 4) that cities can use to tailor their co-creation projects to the contexts in which they are embedded. The framework builds on insights offered by Service Design, Living Labs and Design-Driven Innovation. The 6C Framework distills and expands on the core principles of these three approaches, and is a useful guide for co-creators operating at different levels of governance. It offers a shared language and understanding of the foundational mechanisms for producing public value that can be internalised by stakeholders from all walks of life.

Chapter 4 – Numerous tools are available for co-creation, and their availability is both helpful and confusing. Cities need guidance on what tools to use, in which context, and at what phase of the co-creation project. This chapter does just that. Here, a concise and clear roadmap for implementing co-creation in cities is presented. The roadmap follows a series of specific phases, spanning from exploration to dissemination, and sub-activities within which several potential tools to be applied are mentioned. In this roadmap, co-creation stages are presented and unpacked. This chapter is a practical intermezzo that bridges theory and practice with a specific flowchart based on the 6C Framework and on practical insights, to kick-off value co-creation with and by PSOs.

Chapter 5 – But how does this really work in practice? To answer this question and to demonstrate how the tools and principles previously presented can be deployed, Chapter 5 provides the descriptions and testimonials of various co-creation projects. The wide array of projects featured span across multiple approaches, methods, and combinations of stakeholder groups. Leveraging the testimonials and a literature review, we address the question, 'Why do local city governments decide to co-create with citizens, and which barriers may hamper the adoption of co-creation?' We show that while the gains of co-creation may seem obvious, they cannot be taken for granted. In particular, the testimonials offer some key learning points that can be extracted from past and current examples in Europe that can be used in future endeavours.

Chapter 6 – This chapter sheds light on the organisational transformation of city administrations in relation to co-creation. In particular, internal structures and intrinsic culture present enablers and barriers when institutionalising the involvement of various stakeholders, including citizens. The goal is to help PSOs tackle questions about their intra-organisational focus but also about inter-organisational relationships. For this purpose, we introduce the *Co-creation Readiness Compass,* which can be used as guidance in strategising public value co-creation, shaping of the authorising environment and operational capacity building.

Afterword – Here, we summarise the main contributions of this book before offering a view on what lies on the horizon for co-creation. We envision co-creation where technology is used in service of society, and not as an end goal itself. In delineating a relational view of the citizen, we propose that the solutions to the varied wicked problems that plague local governments lie in a radical transformation in our viewpoints, beliefs and culture.

NOTE

1. Insights are based on interviews with several European cities (so-called 'reference zones') asking about co-creation needs and guidance prior to conducting pilot studies in a multi-stakeholder setting. See SynchroniCity: Delivering an IoT enabled Digital Single Market for Europe and Beyond which received funding from the European Union's Horizon 2020 research and innovation programme under grant agreement no. 732240 (2017–2020).

Chapter 2

CO-CREATION AND THE CITY

> It is an undeniable reality that in today's network and information society people are both more assertive and more independent than in the past. This, combined with the need to reduce the budget deficit, means that the classical welfare state is slowly but surely evolving into a participation society. Everyone who is able will be asked to take responsibility for their own lives and immediate surroundings. When people shape their own futures, they add value not only to their own lives but to society as a whole. (Speech from the Throne 2013)[1]

Citizenship is a concept that is currently being revised (Eizaguirre, Pradel-Miquel, & García, 2017; Kitchin et al., 2019). Citizens are more actively participating in society and, as a result, their relationship with the public sector is also evolving. On the one hand, public-sector reforms that decrease welfare entitlements place greater responsibility on citizens to secure public goods and services on their own. At the same time, citizens are being recruited by the public sector to more actively contribute to the governance (Buijs et al., 2019). Through their participation in public fora, citizens may increase their capacity for self-organisation, which in turn increases their capacity to solve shared problems on their own, from the bottom up. At the same time, those who are participating are reshaping the relationship between the public and the government, with important implications for government and governance (Holm & Berardo, 2020; Nguyen Long, Foster, & Arnold, 2019). A number of tools, methods, and frameworks have emerged to enable collaboration between the public and government (Ansell & Gash, 2008), and also to study it (cf. Ansell, Doberstein, Henderson, Siddiki, & 't Hart, 2020). One of the main findings of these studies is that not all citizens have the ability, desire, or opportunity to engage in this so-called 'participation society' (Koster, 2014). Therefore, the factors which promote and hinder their participation must be carefully interrogated.

The idea of participation is far from new, but it has become a compelling subject for public scrutiny. In recent years, the term has, particularly, been used in developing a framework to understand how the changing media and communication environment is facilitating (or, hindering) participation in society (van der Graaf, 2020). In fact, 'participation' has been conceptualised as 'the state of being related to a larger whole' (*The Merriam-Webster Dictionary*), and 'the process or fact of sharing in an action, sentiment, etc.; active involvement in a matter or event, especially one in which the outcome directly affects those taking part' (*The Oxford English Dictionary*). The term captures taking part in something, fosters certain interests and is never a fully individual act, as such indicating a more normative agenda (Livingstone, 2013). The literature on participation has generated many positions but, arguably, can be demonstrated by a sociological and a political approach. From the former stance, participation is about taking part in particular social processes associated with various kinds of simultaneous and dynamic human to human, human to technology, and human to idea interactions, while the political approach points to the power dynamics that may drive decision-making, and ways to diminish or offset these power imbalances (Carpentier, 2016). As promoters of 'cultures of participation', what these perspectives have in common, is being collaborative in principle and, increasingly, networked in technology and 'peer-to-peer', or multi-stakeholder in organisation. In this view, today's media and tech environment is said to reshape the 'opportunity structures' by which people can take part in a progressively mediatised society (Cammaerts, 2012).

The participation concept has gained renewed momentum as evidenced by the so-called 'participatory turn' associated with the Web 2.0, which offers users an easy-to-use creative infrastructure to actively engage in digital development practices. In other words, so-called participatory activities have drawn specific attention to the parameters underpinning media design and use (extending the conceptualisation of active audiences; Livingstone, 2003), especially, as users of and participants in online content production (or, user-generated content). In addition to the production of meanings, users actively engage in shaping, altering, and distributing media texts, or content (cf. Burgess, 2007; Jenkins, 2006). In this way, users – though not all, and not equally – are invited to produce, change, and share digital content (or, data) as well as also draw in and engage with their own 'public' on platforms such as Instagram. The processes of participation (and, arguably, of democracy) are thus increasingly shaped by information and communication technologies and point to a move away from industrial practices towards 'user-led online environments', captured by terms such as 'pro-am' (Leadbeater & Miller, 2004), 'convergence culture' (Jenkins, 2006); 'culture of connectivity' (van Dijck, 2013); 'produsage' (Bruns, 2008); 'prosumption' (Ritzer & Jurgenson, 2010). Moreover, these user-led sites seem to underpin an information-based model rather than a trichotomous industrial model of production, distribution, and consumption. From this viewpoint, the status of the product (as information and/or intangible) is understood as a dynamic that is collaboratively produced by participants who are all producers and users of information and knowledge, thereby highlighting a shift in connection between 'consumption and production' towards a multi-stakeholder perspective (van der Graaf, 2018a).

The 'participatory' trajectory has thus become an important term in developing a framework to understand emergent media and tech practices (sociological view) as well as an essential component of planning and policy making processes (political perspective), thereby it is increasingly associated terms, particularly, co-creation has gained prominence. Co-creation is a rather ancient and under documented practice, and today, resides within a divergent ecosystem of practitioners and knowledge systems (Cizek & Uricchio, 2019). While the terms co-creation and (public) participation have, at times, been used interchangeably, co-creation is distinct from participation in a variety of ways.

More specifically, co-creation allows citizens from a wide cross-section of communities to proactively contribute to a changing organisational culture. Rather than simply treating citizens as repositories of information about the services they use, co-creation allows them to steer the creative process, generate tools and information, and self-organise and govern. The many tools and methods – which may be supported by technologies – used in co-creation can help hasten the development process, while empowering citizens to productively collaborate with partners even at a distance. With co-creation, different types of value can be created for different stakeholders, depending on their level of involvement, interest, and influence. Furthermore, co-creation aimed at an output that is carried by many and long-lasting (or, 'sustainable') should be a systemic (and not a linear) process underpinning scale level, city politics and characteristics of the socio-technical system associated with a multi-stakeholder ecosystem (cf. Solman, Smits, van Vliet, & Bush, 2021). The objective is thus to yield insights into what co-creation is and may mean in an urban governance setting for a sustainable outlook on cities.

The structure of the remainder of this chapter is as follows: First, a reflection is offered on the term and deployment of co-creation and adjacent terms, such as co-production, co-design and user-driven innovation recognising different conceptual views in different disciplines. This is followed by positioning co-creation in the public service-sector context of city governance, which explores the evolution of the relationship between citizens and public service organisations (PSOs). In doing so, mutual dependencies between the city and other stakeholders, especially citizens, are made apparent and comprehensible. We embed this discussion in an exploration of the central challenges experienced by PSOs embarking on public value co-creation, thereby directing the current debate on public-sector transformation from tactical responses towards a more systemic, value-based approach. This, as we argue, has potential socio-economic and environmental impacts on how we deliver better urban living conditions in the long term.

2.1. CO-CREATION IN PERSPECTIVE

> People act in all kinds of ways, for better or for worse, and generally society considers that a matter of individual freedom. But when people participate in something, society tends to judge whether such participation is beneficial to the participants and/or the wider public, and it may provide public funding or other institutional support [...]. (Livingstone, 2013, p. 24)

For government leaders and PSOs, such as city authorities, more specifically, citizen participation facilitates the identification and acquisition of insights, such as about community needs, attitudes and opinions, new ideas, as well as permits easier implementation, and forges constituency support. From a citizen or communal stance, the participation premise holds the opportunity to claim their political rights and to have their needs and preferences represented by public-sector decision-making about the planning and policymaking processes. Within these views, increasingly, the term co-creation can be detected, which 'implies more than asking citizens just to participate in the production of public services' (Voorberg, Bekkers, Timeus, Tonurist, & Tummers, 2017, p. 178). This stresses beneficial outcomes when citizens are part of the public services design process.

Co-creation's origin cannot be easily determined. Interestingly, the *Oxford English Dictionary* returns no previous uses and, hence, no definitions of co-creation, while – the contested – Google Ngram Viewer registers the term as early as the mid-nineteenth century, and was steadily used after the 1960s, yet its deployment can be seen to escalate from 2004 upwards. Links include marketing, management, tech entrepreneurship, social movements and so forth as well as terms such as collaboration and grassroots. Notwithstanding some semantic slippage, co-creation seems to overlap with, and diverge, from other concepts (such as co-design, co-production, co-construction, user-driven innovation) deployed in various fields (Cizek & Uricchio, 2019).

One stream of thought concerns business and marketing research connecting co-creation with the integration of 'consumers' in the supply chain for reasons such as cost minimisation, increased customer satisfaction and product/service differentiation (Vargo & Lusch, 2004). More specifically, co-creation allows consumers to have influence over the production process and design of the final product, which is expected to generate a significant increase in the demand for the product, thereby raising its economic worth. In particular, Prahalad and Ramaswamy (2000, 2004) have devised the concept 'value co-creation' to position consumers as users, a lens that orients the design, production, and marketing of products and services around people's preferences, values, and needs. Value co-creation, then, results from the purposeful engagement of customers desiring to improve how a product or service is experienced by the user (De Koning, Crul, & Wever, 2016). Under this view, consumers are transformed into active contributors, or co-creators, who cultivate value in a product or service, so that they can exploit it (Brandsen, Steen, & Verschuere, 2018; Payne, Storbacka, & Frow, 2008), and which is associated with a service-dominant logic (in contrast to a goods dominant logic) (cf. Vargo & Lusch, 2008).

In defining co-creation, however, management gurus seem to have married former foes' production and consumption whereby they have sought to carefully avoid the language of labour economics and consumer markets (Van Dijck & Nieborg, 2009). Instead, co-creating communities are depicted as being composed of people who voluntarily participate in these collective initiatives, regardless of whether companies are there to facilitate their involvement or not. In this way, it is argued, that the co-creation model unseats the top-down model of producer-consumer relationships in tearing down the boundary separating market and civic production processes as well as the ones that separate producers from consumers, while the language of not-for-profit community action is co-opted by profit-motivated action.

Around the same time, a shifting focus could also be detected in the field of design. Here, co-creation is rooted in human-centred design and participatory design, which emerged in the 1970s in Scandinavia, where joint decision-making and work practices associated with automatisation started to receive attention (Huybrechts, Benesch, & Geib, 2017). Participatory design can be understood as a design that has 'a special focus on people participating in the design process as co-designers' (Ehn, 2008, p. 93). People's stake in the design process and its results are recognised, as is the value of their expertise, experience, and knowledge, and they are thus empowered to influence design (Mattelmäki & Sleeswijk-Visser, 2011). Designers place people's needs and preferences at the centre of the design process, and they use co-design to collaborate, and it is the environment within which co-creation is situated.

In yet another alternative view, co-design is a method, one of many, used in co-creation. And in these various views, co-creation is often used interchangeably with other terms such as user-generated content, co-production, collaborative or user-driven innovation. For example, YouTube's motto 'Broadcast Yourself' has aptly encapsulated user-generated content by the uploading, viewing, and sharing of videos among users. The impetus for which, arguably, was spearheaded by the open source model of software development associated with the bazaar and gift-giving models (Benkler, 2006; Raymond, 1999). This emergent and rapidly evolving user-generated development has been said to be reflected in the claimed democratisation of Web technologies (van der Graaf, 2018a). With the availability of affordable and accessible tools for content production and distribution, content creation emerged as a creative infrastructure that is associated with pervasive knowledge-intensive and information-rich collaboration practices.

Voorberg, Bekkers, and Tummers (2015) observe that both co-creation and co-production are largely defined in similar terms and empirically used as interchangeable concepts, yet that if any difference can be distilled, it is the insistence of co-creation as value. Furthermore, in the innovation studies literature, the user-centred innovation perspective acknowledges the creative capacity of individuals, highlighting that organisation-user interactions can lead to successful innovation when, occasionally, users contribute to, or augment, organisation-developed products and services (Chesbrough, Vanhaverbeke, & West, 2006; von Hippel, 2005). As a result, the innovation process is said to have become increasingly 'democratized' (von Hippel, 2005).

Following this line of argument, organisations appear to be actively encouraging and facilitating users in the innovation process as suggested by their provision of purposefully designed and provided toolkits. Providing toolkits is a means of systematically outsourcing certain design and innovation tasks from the company to the user, assisting users in activities such as developing customisations and solutions. From this toolkit approach to user-driven innovation, PSOs may benefit from a relatively low-cost approach to acquiring user-provided information, generating new ideas and detecting and solving problems in user creation practices. This perspective can inform the investigation of internal and external knowledge flows across organisational boundaries with the aim of highlighting users as external resources that may benefit product and service development (cf. Foray, 2004). From this innovation lens, co-creation guided by toolkits may provide the organisation with opportunities to learn from (and possibly monetise) the acquisition of information associated with its products and services, tailoring them to specific needs of users and contributing to the overall knowledge base of the organisation (van der Graaf, 2018a).

Over the past decades, these and other terms have appeared widely in scientific literature across various disciplines showing different versions, or demarcations of how co-creation has been applied (Ramaswamy & Ozcan, 2018). Perhaps unsurprisingly, co-creation has been termed a 'magic concept' (Voorberg et al., 2015). The number of benefits associated with co-creation are manifold. It is described as a catalyst for innovation that is rooted in novel ideas, which can only arise from the collective and collaborative knowledge exchange and generation. In addition to the qualitative leap in information and ideas, co-creation reduces risk by raising customer satisfaction, which can cement the relationship between customer and producer, generates more positive testimonials, and increases speed of implementation (e.g., community, market). Co-creation is said to spark change, by itself evolving as it gains meaning for participants who value its openness, diversity, and the space it provides to their voice (cf. Leino & Puumala, 2021).

Yet, because co-creation is described across various fields and practical applications, there is not a fixed framework or method to follow, which is what this book seeks to remedy in the urban context (cf. De Koning et al., 2016). In following Cizek and Uricchio (2019), we propose, that in its core, co-creation is relational, subscribes to a collective sense of ownership, evolves out of process within stakeholder communities and, at present, primarily occurs with people (but it is anticipated, increasingly, also with non-human systems). In doing so, 'co-creation reframes the ethics of who creates, how, and why [it] interprets the world and seeks to change it through a lens of equity and justice' (Cizek & Uricchio, 2019, np).

2.2. VALUE CO-CREATION IN PUBLIC-SECTOR ORGANISATIONS: A CURRENT 'STATE OF AFFAIRS'

The last five decades has seen an evolution in mindset about how the citizen and public administration relate to one another. For over five decades, a struggle has been underway to introduce more balance in the power-relationship between public authorities and citizens. And this shift in mindset underpins the development of citizen-centred public administration.

In many places, the shift towards citizen-centred public administration first began with a shift in thinking towards the citizen-as-customer. In this New

Public Management approach, public administration must meet the demands of citizens by providing a bundle of goods, oftentimes through public-private partnerships. Citizens' role in the process is passive: they influence public administration indirectly, through their choices about which public goods and services to consume, and from whom to procure them. Moreover, PSOs compete with the private sector for the patronage of citizens. Performance is the gold standard of this approach. This standard emphasises citizens' satisfaction and not their responsibility, which leads to an intensification of the claims they make on PSOs. Although this increases the power of the citizen vis-à-vis the government, the dichotomy of public service provider and public service consumer is maintained, and the opportunity to leverage citizen knowledge and creativity is missed.

As the drawbacks of this approach became apparent and difficult to ignore, particularly the strain that it places on public services, the mindset on the relationship between citizens and PSOs once again shifted. In this new view, neither PSOs nor citizens dominate the relationship, rather they partner and share responsibility for creating public goods and services. Citizens work with the government alongside other stakeholders to jointly solve shared problems. They remain at the centre of this paradigm, but this time the emphasis is on their contribution to the public good. Co-creation is the end goal of this new face of public administration embodied by New Public Governance where it is deployed to tackle complex and wicked societal problems (Head & Alford, 2015).

What we now refer to as 'co-creation' has, to some extent, been in practice for a while in territories where the institutional infrastructure supports and encourages a continuous dialogue between public authorities, civil society, and citizens. At the same time, the need for public-sector innovations that can raise city administrations' capacity to meet the many complex governance challenges of this era is intensifying. In consequence, PSOs are increasingly adopting co-creation to collaborate with diverse actors, particularly citizens, in these efforts to develop new public solutions. Beyond markets and governments, co-creation leverages a new value production paradigm which harnesses the creative potential of multi-actor collaboration throughout the policy cycle (Nabatchi, Sancino, & Sicilia, 2017).

The term co-creation was developed in the private sector where the focus has been on maximising service satisfaction associated with market shares and profits, yet the notion is also relevant to the public sector. PSOs are occupied with supplying services characterised by simultaneous production and consumption processes centred around service recipients, which make them ideal for co-creation (Osborne & Strokosch, 2013). Here, value co-creation does not lie with the PSOs or the (service) user rather it being 'a fluid and heterogeneous process that is subjective, contextual, and temporal [...] the value co-creation process will involve different elements in differing relationships to one another for different types of PSO and the different services they offer, characterised by multiplicity'(Cluley & Radnor, 2020, p. 216; see also Chapter 6). More specifically, co-creation in the public-sector context is understood

> as a process through which two or more public and private actors attempt to solve a shared problem, challenge, or task through a constructive exchange of different kinds of knowledge, resources, competences, and ideas that enhance the production of public value in terms of visions, plans, policies, strategies, regulatory frameworks, or services, either through a continuous improvement of outputs or outcomes or through innovative step-changes that transform the understanding of the problem or task at hand and lead to new ways of solving it. (Torfing, Sørensen, & Røiseland, 2019, p. 802)

This multi-stakeholder ecosystem[2] is populated by public actors (e.g., politicians, public managers, and street-level bureaucrats) and private actors (e.g., citizens, community and voluntary groups, corporations, etc.) whose simultaneous interactions give rise to the structure of the ecosystem.

Notably, the discourse around co-creation ascribes a central role to citizens in the co-creation process (cf. Nederhand & van Meerkerk, 2017). Citizens are described as engines of innovation, and their participation is seen as bolstering the representativeness of the democratic underpinnings of public service provision. Their participation has been substantially facilitated by digitalisation and the emergence of new concepts like 'smart cities' and 'smart citizens'. While there are reasons to doubt that the complexity and intractability of today's urban problems can be resolved through participatory citizenship alone, the notion of citizens engaging actively in governance gains salience when one considers the critical interdependencies that give rise to those problems. These interdependencies suggest that solutions should be co-created with all stakeholders with access to the knowledge, resources, and abilities needed to generate new, transformative ideas. This view on citizenship builds on a long tradition that first arose from urban planning and development research and has since evolved and given rise to many different modalities for citizen participation. However, the level of inclusivity and engagement of citizens in so-called participatory governance processes varies substantially.

Sherry Arnstein's (1969) seminal metaphor of a ladder, wherein the intensity of engagement rises as one climbs the rungs of a ladder which leads from passivity to self-governance, is a good tool for examining variation in participation. In the context of co-creation, the extent to which private actors are engaged can vary, lying along a continuum where on one end public administration realises the value of co-creation and aspires to engage and empower citizens and other stakeholders in the process, and begins to take concrete steps in that direction. On the other end of the continuum, what we term 'peak co-creation', all relevant stakeholders jointly set priorities of co-creation and meet them with policy experimentation and collectively take action to scale the resulting policy solutions up, and out.

Co-creation revises and nuances the relationship between the public actors and the private actors. Co-creation creates opportunities to build and sustain more familiar, more creative, more extensive, and more profound relationships compared to other types of interactions between citizens and the public sector. As described by Cottam and Leadbeater (2004, p. 22), co-creation: 'is a more creative and interactive process which challenges the views of all parties and seeks to combine professional and local expertise in new ways'. It empowers private actors to contribute to the provision of public goods and in policymaking, and provides the public sector with a range of new tools and approaches to generate public goods and services (e.g., CitizenLab, bpart platform, Decidim, OpenGov, LiveStories, or specific Living Lab or citizen science portals).[3] This mutually beneficial and symbiotic relationship makes co-creation attractive to many city governments. The mushrooming of urban experiments like Living Labs and citizen juries illustrates cities' commitments to put this concept into practice on the ground. This enthusiasm for using digital tools and approaches to enhance participatory citizenship must be tempered by an awareness that the process can still fail to be sufficiently inclusive. Accordingly, in the next section, attention will be given to the challenges, or 'disenchantment' with co-creation in the urban context (Dudau, Glennon, & Verschuere, 2019).

2.3. CO-CREATION MUSINGS

Cities are actively seeking transformation. Transformation, used in an urban context, emphasises and acknowledges that intractable, coupled, and complex social, ecological, and economic challenges can only be resolved through systemic change (Hölscher & Frantzeskaki, 2021). Ideas about these changes emphasise digital and sustainability transformations, but also fundamental changes in societal organisation. Co-creation is seen as a pathway to develop innovations that can spark a cultural transformation towards a more sustainable and just society (Rossi & Tuurnas, 2021; cf.

'right to the city' and associated terms such as 'spatial justice' in Kitchin et al., 2019). They are drawn towards co-creation by the rhetoric around its promise to overcome resource constraints while simultaneously revitalising democracy by raising public engagement (Ansell & Torfing, 2021) and generating social cohesion through the seeding of co-creation communities (Godinho et al., 2021). Thus, citizens themselves are seen as transforming due to their engagement in co-creation. And, as those who steer these processes, the potential for public-sector transformation is also underlined (Torfing et al., 2019).

Public-sector transformation implies a fundamental change in organisational culture and practice. However, the size and complexity of PSOs, as well as the different logics that drive public administration thinking (March & Olsen, 2004; Simon & Barnard, 1947; Weber, Kopelman, & Messick, 2004) can impede co-creation. The open, networked, and bottom-up design processes that typically define co-creation can stand in stark contrast to hierarchically organised PSOs, and it therefore may face resistance from public actors inculcated in a top-down and siloed bureaucratic culture. Public officials may also be wary of the harm and disruption co-creation may impose on the prevailing ways of working, policies, and programmes. Co-creation can also be burdensome for PSOs: it requires them to become familiar with an extensive governance landscape and keep abreast of all of the pertinent laws, regulations, standards and policies that affect co-creation. The impact of co-creation in the public-sector context is likely to be circumscribed by these factors, among others. Therefore, PSOs' ability to move co-creation from an idea that can take root in practice needs to be examined.

A second barrier to transformation is the limited potentiality ascribed to co-creation. Co-creation in public settings, such as urban development, can be a strategy for addressing complex societal problems, arguably, relating to increasingly strained public budgets, hence, seeking to harness the resources of civil society (Baptista, Alves, & Matos, 2020; Osborne & Strokosch, 2013). In this view, a problem-solving and resource perspective seemingly take precedent over co-creation ideals of inclusion, representation and empowerment (Lund, 2018). Some, such as those who see the 'communicative turn' in planning theory, have called for more sincere and inclusive public participation (Innes & Booher, 2018; cf. Habermas, 1981). It has been observed, however, that in practice the limited nature by which co-creation usually is realised – for example, by means of small-scale experimentation, Living Labs, citizen self-organisation – seem to primarily function as mechanisms to support the public that often systematically exclude marginalised or disadvantaged populations and tend to interact superficially with the public.

Transformative co-creation requires a more involved form of participation. In co-creation, public value creation and innovation is yielded only by collaboration between diverse stakeholders. Therefore, the role that citizens and public authorities play in co-creation must be specified. According to Lund (2018), the opacity about actor roles arises from a prevailing tension between two traditions, which have both contributed to the development of co-creation: participatory democracy and deliberative democracy. Participatory democracy emphasises empowering citizens to control those political and policy decisions in which they have a stake (cf. 'social innovation' in Lund, 2018; Baptista et al., 2020). Instead, deliberative democracy emphasises the need for public discourse and debate on societal challenges. These two aims, that of improving services through a more holistic and citizen-centred decision-making process and that of ensuring that co-creation is an instrument for participatory democracy and institutional legitimisation, can run counter to one another. Both are compromised by biased participation.

Biased participation can result in public services or goods that neglect the needs or even harm segments of a city's residents. Co-creation processes may be organised in ways that are inconvenient, time consuming, overly formal in both process and language, and overlook the contexts in which citizens experience public services. Furthermore, what motivates citizens to participate in co-creation is oftentimes neglected, and as such co-creation will fail to serve as a meaningful tool for inclusive, participatory democracy (Leino & Puumala, 2020). As a result, it can be difficult to shift towards a co-creation mindset, particularly for public servants whose professionalisation and experience hinder necessary behavioural and attitudinal adaptations to co-creation. Some behaviours (e.g., preferences for rigid chains of command and use of formal language) can discourage citizen participation in co-creation (Torfing et al., 2019). As a result, bias is mobilised in favour of participants with a high level of familiarity with and knowledge of these types of processes (cf. Agger, 2012). This has a consequence for how we study and improve co-creation. Instead of understanding how citizens can be supported so that they can actively shape the development of new products or services, actual co-creation practices in a public-sector context are said to concentrate on merely collecting information on citizen satisfaction with public services (cf. Breuer & Pierson, 2021; Kitchin et al., 2019). In these types of set-ups, participation tends to serve the short-term priorities of the public sector, neglect unperceived needs of citizens, and can miss the chance to address long-term societal challenges. While a successful process may yield innovations. In order for those innovations to generate value in practice, there is a need to account for the diversity of public views, needs, and experiences (Leino & Puumala,

2020). Such an accounting is facilitated by prioritising inclusion and learning in co-creation. A key question therefore is access.

Access is deeply related to social justice and citizen's rights to inclusion in the city. Critical voices highlight inequalities in the cities that create parallel lived realities for its inhabitants. The existence of such sharp differences means that co-creation can only capture a subset of residents' lives leaving a substantial knowledge gap. Furthermore, accessibility in co-creation operates at different levels. The first is at the point of entry to co-creation, whereby people who are systematically marginalised, stigmatised, or underprivileged are excluded from co-creation (Leino & Puumala, 2020). Here, in the context of co-creation, it is also important to consider the digital divide and the various intersections of society that it can affect (Effing & Groot, 2016; Shin, Kim, & Chun, 2021). At a deeper level is the lack of accessibility to decision-making within co-creation processes themselves. In democratic fora like referendums or elections, each citizen has an equal level of 'voice' in the process, this expectation does not hold in the context of co-creation (Torfing et al., 2019). Imbalances in representation spill over to implementation, where discussions about implementation results can be stymied by the absence of insight from users from disadvantaged communities.

Nevertheless, co-creation is being used to address a broad swath of policy issues. In order to work, both public and private actors must be capacitated to collaborate in an inclusive and open process (Brandsen, 2021). While private actors may need greater knowledge and skills, public actors will need to learn how to exercise the transformative and facilitative leadership that is necessary for managing a collaborative process (Bryson, Crosby, & Stone, 2015; Budd & Sancino, 2016). These leadership traits are particularly salient when the issues being tackled by public administration are complex and wicked (Head & Alford, 2015). Since these abilities can be gained over time and with experience, co-creation requires learning, both individual and collective. Learning can manifest in different ways and at different parts of the policy process, and it is multi-layered. At the highest layer, learning manifests as policy change, or policy learning (Voorberg et al., 2017). But this type of change is difficult to achieve in a short time, and must be accompanied by changes to the conditions within which policy choices are made including institutional and regulatory frameworks. Therefore, policy change, especially transformative policy change, requires years if not decades to achieve (Baumgartner & Jones, 2010; Weible & Sabatier, 2018). At a second layer, learning happens when individuals change their perspective and are willing to adopt new ideas about an issue, process, or outcome. Voorberg et al. (2017) describe learning in co-creation as a process of frame adaption which allows diverse actors with diverse perspectives to reconcile differences and formulate a coherent, evolved, and shared understanding. This view aligns with other perspectives on group-based learning offered in policy studies, whereby learning is understood as a change in beliefs that occurs when knowledge is updated so that groups with opposing beliefs can meet in the middle (Weible & Sabatier, 2018). This type of collective learning is necessary for initiating policy change and can be defined as:

> a collective process, which may include acquiring information through diverse actions (e.g., trial and error), assessing or translating information, and disseminating knowledge or opportunities across individuals in a collective, and 2) collective products that emerge from the process, such as new shared ideas, strategies, rules, or policies. (Heikkila & Gerlak, 2013, p. 486)

Learning collectively, in an inclusive and collaborative environment where participants are driven by a shared purpose and value system, can drive a system change leading to urban transformation.

The benefits that have been associated with co-creation are manifold. To begin, co-creation may improve public services: it may generate innovations that raise the efficiency and efficacy of current solutions, or address yet unmet needs. At the same time, co-creation has been proposed to improve the democratic quality of public services and their provision by incorporating citizen participation and voice through deliberation. Citizens' trust in public-sector organisations may grow, and they may begin to view them as (more) legitimate. Zooming out from the citizen and into the community, co-creation may also raise trust among citizens, thereby generating social capital and social cohesion. Both social capital and social cohesion have been shown to raise the resilience of communities to external shocks and challenges (Klinenberg, 2015; Wolf, Neil Adger, Lorenzoni, Abrahamson, & Raine, 2010). However, in order to capture all of these benefits, co-creators must mediate a number of risks.

Co-creation involves risks. These risks relate to the inputs and throughputs of co-creation. As described by Scharpf (2015), writing specifically on the subject of legitimacy, input captures the level of citizen representation in a political process, while output captures the extent to which the outcomes of a process satisfy popular will, regardless of the level of citizen input. Schmidt (2013) expands this definition to account for throughput, those procedural standards which are put in place to maintain accountability, transparency, and inclusiveness in governance. As observed by Torfing et al. (2019), co-creation may fail to uphold standards of democratic accountability because it enables non-elected actors to make decisions that affect the public. Moreover, in co-creation, public-sector organisations and societal entities whose role it is to hold PSOs to account work together with them, which makes them even less likely to perform this role (Larsson, 2019). Co-creation can also be expensive and challenging to put into action, especially when the goals and expectations of different participants do not align. Finally, there is a biased participation which, as described previously, leads to the over-representation of some voices, and the under-representation if not complete exclusion of others. Problems with inputs and throughput necessarily have an impact on output, or the outcomes of co-creation (Bentzen, 2020). It is possible that the outcomes will be undesirable, as a result of the presence of one or more of the risks described previously. First, goal misalignment combined with a failure to moderate or facilitate consensus can lead to the adoption of choices as a compromise, rather than as an effort to optimise. It may also stir deep and irreconcilable conflicts among participants. In the face of a lack of accountability and/or biased participation, the result of co-creation may simply be symbolic, or worse it may impose the burden of realising public goods and services onto vulnerable communities. Managing these risks is a core challenge of co-creation in the public sector.

Although co-creation entails numerous challenges, it still holds the potential to improve, if not transform, the public sector and the city itself. However, this potential can only be realised if citizens are included from the process outset, and if their inclusion is sustained through continuous co-creation. We argue that it is therefore important to be mindful of the inter-relationship between input, throughput, and output in co-creation. This mindfulness is enabled when co-creators think of the co-creation sequentially. Contemplating and considering how all stakeholders, particularly citizens, can be engaged at each phase of co-creation can help ensure that the engagement of diverse stakeholders is meaningful from decision-making, all the way to implementation, monitoring, and evaluation. In other words, co-creation is continuous (Bentzen, 2020). Citizens and other stakeholders need to be involved in co-creation from the very beginning. In order to nourish the trust built in the process of co-creation and maintain momentum all the way to the implementation of the policy or programme, private actors – especially citizens – need to continuously be involved throughout the process, in order to ensure that it does not lose steam and end prematurely (Bentzen, 2020). This means being willing to reckon with new, sometimes distressing knowledge, and to maintain an open mindset nevertheless. This requires a shift in thinking.

Adopting a co-creation mindset involves a commitment to transform organisational culture. To begin, the logics of top-down command and control systems of action must be replaced by horizontal, non-hierarchical organisation where PSOs steer the process rather than to control it (Kassim & Le Galès, 2010). This provides a more welcoming environment where citizens can flourish. Second, PSOs must be open to a cultural evolution that emphasises deliberation, openness, and the desire to learn. Moreover, participants must abandon short-term thinking for a long-term vision. In making this shift, PSOs embrace novelty, experimentation, and even small failures which can lead to great gains of knowledge. Additionally, PSOs may more thoroughly exploit the digital transformation as a means of connecting citizens to public service and allowing them to work collaboratively. In their participation in co-creation, citizens link the inputs of the process (to which they actively contribute) to its output (which they most likely will use). These changes should allow for more meaningful collaboration between citizens and the government (such as in the redesign of public squares, green playgrounds, safe crossroads, public arts designs, and so forth). Governments gain in terms of legitimacy, public trust, and innovation. Instead, citizens can increase their sense of belonging in the city, and are empowered to contribute to the sustainability of that very city.

NOTES

1. His Majesty King Willem-Alexander, Speech from the Throne 2013. See https://www.royal-house.nl/documents/speeches/2013/09/17/speech-from-the-throne-2013. Accessed on June 14, 2021.

2. Note that in this understanding, the term seems to bear some resemblance to 'social innovation' and 'collaborative governance'. Yet, through the former civil society fills the gaps in services left by private industry and the public sector. Instead, co-creation unites these three spheres in a collaborative environment which enables learning, experimentation, and the formulation of multiple possible solutions to a shared problem.

3. See respectively, https://www.citizenlab.co/; https://bpart.be/ ; https://decidim.org/; https://opengov.com/; https://www.livestories.com/about; https://enoll.org/; and, https://www.zooniverse.org/

Chapter 3

DESIGN PRINCIPLES FOR CO-CREATING
IN AND WITH CITIES

Cities interested in co-creation may be confronted with several challenges. To begin, reaching out to and effectively engaging with users is neither simple nor is it without costs. Furthermore, organising co-creation activities with new actors, in virtual communities, to effectively deliver what has been co-designed or agreed on can be difficult (Spagnoli et al., 2019). Each city will have specific needs and faces different challenges. For this reason, the co-creation approaches and services that a city administration can consider must be tailored specifically to that focal city or region's socio-cultural, economic, and technological contexts. In other words, the outcome of the co-creation process critically hinges on *how* things are designed in that process, and the appropriate method will vary from context to context. A first step in this direction is to identify core principles of the design process, which through their recombination can constitute a public-sector co-creation approach that is customised to the local contexts and global environments within which a city operates.

This chapter provides a baseline conceptualisation of several design approaches and principles for effectively enacting co-creation in different local contexts. Practical design principles are necessary to successfully execute a co-creation process. Accordingly, this chapter offers a series of six guiding principles ('6C Framework') for concretely and effectively enacting co-creation with citizens. These guiding principles support the identification of a set of methods and tools (presented in more detail in Chapter 4) that cities can use to exploit co-creation approaches in a practical and tailored way. These guiding principles build on insights offered by Service Design, Living Labs, and Design-Driven Innovation. Given that the field of co-creation is wide and diverse, the aim here is not to offer an extensive literature review of all the available approaches. Rather, the goal is to provide guidelines that can be used for a range of purposes when co-creating with citizens (and other stakeholders) in cities. We achieve this by distilling and discussing the core principles of these three approaches, and then synthesising them into the six guiding principles presented at the end of this chapter.

3.1. OVERCOMING VALUE CO-CREATION CHALLENGES WITH DESIGN PRINCIPLES

Public-sector organisations (PSOs), particularly city governments, can greatly benefit from co-creation with citizens. Citizens are 'providers of added value' whose engagement can improve decision-making processes and public service development and delivery. As suggested in studies of 'smart citizenship', citizens can leverage digital tools to play a more consequential role in society. Indeed, studies of 'citizen sourcing' observe that citizens can shape policy by using digital platforms to share ideas that can contribute to the creation of new services, which can in turn improve deliberative democracy and increase government transparency (Schmidthuber & Hilgers, 2018; Spagnoli et al., 2019). Citizen participation is, however, only a necessary but not a sufficient condition for successful co-creation.

Co-creation can also fail. Indeed, without crucial design principles, co-creation can be more harmful than helpful. Järvi, Kähkönen, and Torvinen (2018) go as far as to call failed co-creation processes and value co-destruction. When it comes to public services, public value co-destruction occurs when the public's involvement promotes public service failure. Irvin and Stansbury (2004, pp. 59–60) coin the phrase 'the power of bad decisions' to describe situations where poor and harmful policy choices are legitimised only because the public was present and consented. In another example, public value co-destruction may happen when a process seems to lack transparency or when there is a miscommunication, which generates distrust and the subsequent misuse or underuse of the resulting public services. The damage done by public value co-destruction is not necessarily limited to the good or service that is being co-created: distrust in the co-creation process can beget more generalised mistrust towards city government. In sum, counter-productive relationships between the various stakeholders of co-creation give rise to public value co-destruction. There are a few core reasons behind public value co-destruction, most of which are rooted in cooperation dilemmas arising from the difficulty in managing diverse stakeholders.

Diversity is both a burden and a boon to the co-creation process. That is, co-creation leverages a multi-stakeholder perspective to overcome disciplinary blindspots. Such an approach, however, faces a range of obstacles (Brewer, 1999; Mazzocchi, 2019) that can manifest at different levels and points of the co-creation process. It can be hindered by differences in cultures, frames of references, interests, aims, disciplinary methodological and epistemic orientations, and personalities of participants. The difficulties involved in managing such a multi-stakeholder process is one of the reasons for which, despite its known benefits, co-creation is not as diffuse a practice as it could be.

Co-creation can also be risky (cf. Chapter 2). Torfing et al. (2019) enumerate the various risks that are associated with co-creation, including biased participation (Turnhout, Van Bommel, & Aarts, 2010.) that privileges either the most extreme or advantaged viewpoints, shortfalls in democratic accountability and transparency due to the participation of non-elected actors in policy making, and the substantial potential for conflict. Additionally, co-creation can also, according to the authors, be merely tokenistic or symbolic, and be incapable of producing any substantive impacts. In this latter case, efforts at co-creation may be diminished to 'talking shops', which delay rather than facilitate necessary action. In part, all of these problems stem from the different levels of resources, power, and influence among participants. Inequalities in power and privilege are common to all participatory and collaborative processes, and they must be addressed carefully through the design of participatory institutions (Fung, 2006, 2015). In terms of accountability, Larsson (2019) warns of the potential for misuse or abuse of power that arises when the very actors who conventionally hold PSOs to account (the public and civil society) become their partners. Another hurdle is the inability to enter into a co-creation mindset: actors who are accustomed to playing conventional roles may resist the new ways of thinking and doing, which are necessary for co-creation (Torfing et al., 2019). Thus, co-creation needs to consider design in order to avoid superficiality in interaction, account for and correct power imbalances, and institute appropriate checks and balances, which do not stymie creativity.

Design principles can help prevent value co-destruction. They achieve this by addressing fundamental challenges that arise from diversity of stakeholders, and the power imbalances between them. Therefore, design principles need to consider (1) knowledge and knowledge sharing; (2) trust among participants; (3) inflexibility; and (4) goal misalignment (Järvi et al., 2018; Torfing et al., 2019). In accounting for design, the term co-creation can be used to mark, respectively, the co-creation spectrum, the co-creation types, the co-creation steps and the joint space of co-creation (Spagnoli et al., 2019). In general, co-creation can be considered both as an innovation approach, as well as materialised in an iterative approach, which follows an extended process based on sharing ideas, combining and selecting them, and starting again with the process (Spagnoli et al., 2019). Thinking in terms of design can encourage interactions which generate trust among participants. Trust is essential for knowledge sharing (Cho & Poister, 2013; Hasche, Höglund, & Mårtensson, 2020). Trust is known to be particularly important for sharing difficult but crucial information which can be important for avoiding mistakes and errors (Costigan, Iiter, & Jason Berman, 1998; Morrow, Hansen, & Pearson, 2004). Trust rises as citizens are more informed about public activities and insights into developments (Hilgers & Ihl, 2010). The use of design principles can also address the need to establish consensus about an initiative's goals in order to mitigate conflict and mistrust. Design principles provide guidance to co-creation processes that can address these needs. They raise the capacity of PSOs to learn from their environment and to use that new knowledge to either improve or innovate. Ideally, design principles should specify the *who* of co-creation (that is, which actors are engaged, and describes their roles in the process), the *what* and *how* (the process), and the *why* (the values being pursued) of value co-creation. By providing answers to these core questions, principles offer guidance on the main inputs and outputs of co-creation.

Co-creation vis-à-vis the conceptualisation of and deployment in design principles encompasses a multitude of definitions posited across disciplines, such as co-design, participatory design and open innovation. For instance, De Koning et al. (2016) provide an analysis of 50 co-creation methods and definitions, presenting a comprehensive analysis of this concept. The result of this work clearly shows that while co-creation has been linked to several applications, a complete and coherent framework is still lacking (De Koning et al., 2016). But it is possible to find common features across co-creation methods. Here, we take a close look at three prominent approaches to designing co-creation processes for value generation, namely: Service Design, Living Labs, and Design-Driven Innovation. These approaches have their strengths and weaknesses, and essentially hold great complementarities, which can be exploited to develop an integrative framework. But first, insights from each approach need to be extracted and refined.

Service Design

Service Design is a broad discipline that was originally conceived in the context of service blueprint design (Shostack, 1982) as a tool for generating new ideas and service concepts. This approach organises services and their provision around how users relate to one another, services, technologies, and PSOs. It leverages a multidisciplinary approach that is crucial for enacting service innovation as it can bring new ideas to life (Ostrom, Parasuraman, Bowen, Patrício, & Voss, 2015). More generally, Service Design connects several valuable contributions to generate new and improved knowledge, such as the customer's value proposition (Edvardsson, Gustafsson, Sandén, & Johnson, 2000), service interfaces that embody service offerings (Secomandi & Snelders, 2011), service operations (Victorino et al., 2018) and supportive technologies that empower service innovation (Kieliszewski, Maglio, & Cefkin, 2012). Thus, Service Design embodies a range of methods and approaches that can be deployed in the process of collaborative knowledge generation.

Service Design finds its roots in Design Research and Marketing. Design research involves the formulation and testing of a design in a real-world setting, so that its weaknesses may be revealed and acted upon through progressive refinement (Collins, Joseph, & Bielaczyc, 2004). Through progressive refinement, the design process itself is put in use to advance research aims (Edelson, 2002). It encompasses four steps: namely (1) research clarification, which involves the formulation of a worthwhile research goal by means of a literature review; (2) descriptive study I, which involves an empirical data analysis embedded in an exploratory study; (3) prescriptive study, or the synthesis of experience into a vision of how to improve upon the existing situation; and (4) descriptive study II, wherein one undertakes empirical data analysis to study the impact of the intervention that was developed in previous rounds (Blessing & Chakrabarti, 2009; Pahl, Beitz, Feldhusen, & Grote, 2007). An interest in this facet has been renewed within the context of 'service research', with a focus on user needs both at the business and societal levels (Patricio, Pinho, Teixeira, & Fisk, 2018). Service Design can be understood as a result of this interest.

Today, there is no universally accepted definition for the Service Design. However, the description of The Copenhagen Institute of Interaction Design can provide a useful summary:

> Service Design is an emerging field focused on the creation of well thought through experiences using a combination of intangible and tangible mediums. It provides numerous benefits to the end user experience [...]. Service design as a practice generally results in the design of systems and processes aimed at providing a holistic service to the user. This cross-disciplinary practice combines numerous skills in design, management and process engineering. However, consciously designed services that

incorporate new business models are empathetic to user needs and attempt to create new socio-economic value in society. Service design is essential in a knowledge driven economy. (as cited in Schneider & Stickdorn, 2011, p. 23)

This definition emphasises that Service Design is essentially a multi-method, transdisciplinary approach which aims to generate new knowledge, which can then be used to design goods and services that provide a holistic end-user experience tied to user needs. However, Service Design does not happen serendipitously. Organisations must prepare and plan for it (Malmberg & Wetter-Edman, 2016). More specifically, PSOs must actively consider the needs of citizen users, the particular features of the services being offered, and account for varying levels of contact and interactions provided between PSOs and citizens in service delivery (Karwan & Markland, 2016). In other words, they need to consider core design principles.

Service Design has five core principles (Stickdorn & Schneider, 2014). The first principle is that services should be 'user centered'. Services should be imagined from the service user's perspective rather than that of the engineer, marketer, manager or designer. In practice, this means that the personal habits of the user, as well as their social environment and culture must be accounted for in design. To obtain this type of knowledge about the user, a collaborative relationship must be established with them. To enter into their mindset, the entire interdisciplinary team must adopt users' language. This language provides them with a common point of departure from which they can collaboratively, co-create value. One important benefit that PSOs may draw from citizen involvement in public service co-creation tends to be an increased trust in governmental institutions (Torfing et al., 2019). Citizen participation may also increase access to the market, reduce timing, and risks, and, consequently, improve loyalty (Auh, Bell, McLeod, & Shih, 2007). Actively involving users at co-creation's onset transforms them from 'co-implementers', who only perform some implementation tasks, into 'co-designers' deciding how a service should be designed and/or 'initiators' who trigger themselves an initiative and PSOs follow their approach (Voorberg et al., 2015). However, both citizens and PSOs need to find the right process for enacting co-creation trajectories, to ensure transparency and trust, and ultimately capture these benefits.

The remaining four principles centre on the Service Design process. The second principle is that Service Design must from its inception be 'co-creative', which means the inclusion and involvement of all relevant stakeholders. Co-creation activities must establish an environment that facilitates the generation and evaluation of ideas within heterogeneous groups, by using mechanisms that promote such creative exchanges. At a minimum, all stakeholders must be able to see and appreciate the value that their participation brings not only to the service, but also to themselves personally. The next core principle is called 'sequencing'. Service Design involves a sequence, or series of interrelated actions, from a pre-service period (perceiving the need to use a service), over the actual service period (using the service), to the post-service period (the user evaluates the service and, hopefully, comes back). By breaking the process up into sequences, participants are better able to orient themselves within the process, while remaining aware of other parts of the sequence (that come after or before) and understand how the current process comes from or contributes to those other stages. By accounting for all of these sequences in the design process – also, through prototyping and iterative testing – an excellent service performance can be achieved. Fourth, is 'evidencing' which can make the different processes tangible or perceptible to users. Physical evidence (e.g., emails, brochures, signs, and souvenirs) helps stakeholders create an emotional connection to the process and amplify their experience of the service. Visualising them can increase user appreciation of the service experience and thus increase their loyalty. The final core principle is that Service Design must be 'holistic'. The entire context – or environment – of a service needs thus to be considered, which is achieved by including all of the different disciplines and ideas that shape that environment. A first step towards this is to integrate the previous principles, that is, user-centred, co-creative processes involving sequencing and evidencing, into one cohesive and coherent experience.

The contributions offered by Service Design to co-creation are clear. They clearly place citizens-as-users' needs and expectations at the forefront and make the fulfilment of those needs the main aim of the process. Additionally, in adopting the citizens-as-users language, Service Design can overcome some challenges common to co-creation, such as competition between disciplinary approaches and misunderstanding. However, these Service Design principles are not without their caveats. To begin, it is very values agnostic, which probably stems from its origins in marketing. While being devoid of a values orientation gives it flexibility to Service Design, it is a weak point when it comes to generating 'public value', which has a philosophical anchoring that is distinct from private value. Importantly, PSOs are distinguished from other types of organisations by their mandate, their need to remain accountable to their constituents, and promote social equity and other public values (Karwan & Markland, 2016). In other words, they must contemporaneously deal with questions of efficiency, effectiveness, and equity, and these goals must orient action and mindsets in public value co-creation.

Living Labs

A complementary perspective to Service Design has been recently provided by the 'Living Labs' community. As a concept and practice, Living Labs emerged contemporaneously with and benefitted from the emergence of social media and Web 2.0. In Living Labs, online activity that is at both times social and creative are harnessed to generate innovations (Schuurman, Baccarne, De Marez, Veeckman, & Ballon, 2016). While Living Labs can mean different things, often it is used to refer to a methodology and open innovation environment for value creation following a what has been termed 'quadruple-helix' process (Borghys, van der Graaf, Walravens, & Van Compernolle, 2020). It emphasises the deep involvement of all relevant stakeholders from academia, businesses, government and citizens in the development of new services, from the idea generation phase all the way through to the evaluation of its impact at both societal and economic level.

Living Labs refer to user-centred, open innovation ecosystems based on a systematic user co-creation approach, integrating research and innovation processes in real-life communities and settings. They operate on multiple scales, including the macro-, or organisational level, which links actors across the territory in co-creation, the meso-level involving activities specific to a sector involved in the overall network, and micro level, which centres around the user's engagement in the process (Schuurman et al., 2016). Furthermore, Living Labs encompass societal and technological dimensions simultaneously in a business-citizens and government-academia partnership which underlines its collaborative approach as a 'quadruple helix structure' including citizens, industry, knowledge institutions and municipalities (see for 'Living Lab definitions', Compagnucci, Spigarelli, Coelho, & Duarte, 2021). The Quadruple Helix builds off the Triple Helix structure (Etzkowitz & Leydesdorff, 1995), which describes the ideal environment for innovation as an essentially networked environment structured around collaboration between actors from industry, government, and university. Operating in the triple helix, universities spur on innovation by conducting and communicating path-breaking research, which industry builds on when it engages in strategic partnerships to bring new goods and services to market, and PSOs formulate policies which support and promote knowledge and value generating activities by both sectors. The Quadruple Helix extends the Triple Helix by accounting for the key role played by citizens in the innovation process (Borghys et al., 2020). By including citizens, it is possible to ensure that innovations are sufficiently accessible, align with core societal values, and reflect the interests of the public. Essentially, Living Labs enable the co-creation of integrated solutions with users through disruptive technologies by following the whole innovation life cycle, both raising awareness on developing public services while encouraging citizens to participate in the technical process and implement policy-related agendas. In these initiatives, Living Labs operate as intermediaries between citizens, research organisations, companies, cities and regions for joint value co-creation, rapid prototyping or validation to scale up innovation and businesses.

The Living Labs multi-method approach develops, manages and contributes to co-create and orchestrate local ecosystems by involving multi-stakeholder teams in the design process, fostering inclusion within urban and regional contexts. Living Labs stand on three pillars: the environment within which the Living Lab is situated, the approach which is put into place, and the outcomes of the approach (Veeckman, Schuurman, Leminen, & Westerlund, 2013). These principles of user engagement and co-creation are reinforced by the Living Lab' emphasis on multi-stakeholder participation that in its focus on users, also engages with all relevant stakeholders. The principal elements of this approach are, first and foremost, its emphasis on user engagement whereby users become equal contributors and co-creators. Second is its emphasis on multi-stakeholder participation, which indicates that users are defined not as a homogenous entity but as constituted of different actors who bring many different resources and ideas to the table (and, hence, spurring innovation), but who may also have poorly aligned interests and beliefs (conflict). Thus, the emphasis on collaboration between users and a range of other stakeholders requires mutually valued outcomes among stakeholders. Having a shared purpose, in addition to being able to draw personal benefit from the process, allows stakeholders to overcome conflicts which may arise. Furthermore, Living Labs uses multi-method approaches in a real-life environment that encompasses various combinations of user-centred, co-creation methodologies to best fit their purpose. This includes constant improvement, by means of collective feedback from users at many points in the process, and having a multi-dimensional view on users which allows them to take on the role that is right for the activity, at each stage of the process (Veeckman et al., 2013). In short, the process involves three E's which are the building blocks of the Living Labs concept: Exploration, Experimentation, Evaluation.[1] The Living Lab methodology is, arguably, rather focussed on the design of a specific product or service, while societal or economic challenges active in the society are less analysed or explored in the co-creation process. In this respect, it contrasts with the Design-Driven Innovation approach.

Design-Driven Innovation

Design Thinking is a 'future-oriented' innovation method that is practiced in many different fields (Brenner, Uebernickel, & Abrell, 2016, p. 4). It is one of the many tools that can be used in Service Design. This dynamic and iterative process encompasses a set of problem-solving tools and approaches, which are all used to address human needs (Gottlieb, Wagner, Wagner, & Chan, 2017). Thus, it creates value by first generating value for the public.

Using an iterative approach, Design Thinking leverages synthesis and analysis to enable learning and innovation in co-creation (Brown, 2008). Discovery in Design Thinking unfolds through an open process of exploration, consultation, and observation, which involves multiple stakeholders, and is iterative. Design Thinking also involves sense-making, scenario building, and interpretation of the new knowledge revealed during discovery. By brainstorming and sharing different viewpoints, participants combine and recombine information and knowledge to generate novelty, which they test through experimentation. Monitoring, evaluation, reflexivity, learning, for an evolutionary process to take hold whereby innovation is a continuous rather than a one-shot process. Design Thinking focuses on people's preferences and for the first time transforms the design approach from linear to 'a system of spaces' (Gottlieb et al., 2017). In this view, each design approach must pass through three fundamental phases: (1) inspiration: the circumstances or issues to be addressed in the design thinking process; (2) ideation: the process of idea genesis and testing; and (3) implementation: setting out the path to market or change in the organisation (Gottlieb et al., 2017).

It is especially within the phases of ideation and implementation that the process is clearly not linear. This is, for example, evident in the context of interface design in software development where the user or human-centric approach is prioritised and the iterative approach is a prerequisite. Within this context, 'design-driven innovation' is the only approach that 'makes sense of things' (Krippendorff, 1989), working at the symbolic level, rather than the technical or functional level. This perspective shares several common principles with 'open innovation' in redefining what a product or service can mean for a user (Verganti, 2008). Aptly defined by Chesbrough (2003, p. 43), open innovation:

> means that valuable ideas can come from inside or outside the company and can go to market from inside or outside the company as well. This approach places external ideas and external paths to market on the same level of importance as that reserved for internal ideas and paths to market during the Closed Innovation Era.

The concept, however, is not totally new. It draws from the literature developed mostly in the 1970s on customer and user-driven innovation, open systems and open paradigms (Selden & MacMillan, 2006; von Hippel, 2005), which has attracted scholarly attention (Chesbrough & Bogers, 2014).The Open Innovation literature presents the open processes as a new 'one best way' to innovate and to succeed. It has led to important insights into how organisations use inflows of knowledge to accelerate internal innovation and outflows of knowledge to expand the markets for external use of innovation (Chesbrough, 2006). The Open innovation approach erodes the boundaries of organisations to promote the adoption of innovations from the outside to allow an organisation to mobilise its resources to outsiders (Bogers et al., 2017). In the context of urban governance, where city government is the under-study organisation and citizens are the opted outside stakeholders, the open innovation approach is said to be a valuable source of innovations for value co-creation (von Hippel, 2005). Furthermore, by opening up towards the outsiders, PSOs can be the source of innovations which find their ways to stakeholders through new actors who operate outside traditional government channels. While open innovation is mostly focussed on the source of innovation and innovation adoption/exportation, design thinking highlights the iterations and adaptations required in the innovation process, wherever the innovation originates from.

All of these different methodologies and approaches for enacting service innovation, both at private and public level share some common guiding principles, which are clearly and effectively summarised by the British Design Council's Double Diamond model (Hambeukers, 2019). This model provides a structured process for designing innovation, with a combination between divergent thinking and convergent thinking. In this model, the design process has four different phases, namely (i) discover, (ii) understand, (iii) develop and (iv) deliver.

Furthermore, the core principles of Design-Driven Innovation are, to start with, an understanding of the people using a service, their needs, strengths and aspirations. In other words, it centres on putting people first (associated with user-centred design). As a consequence of this human-centred approach, the design process incorporates interaction, conflict negotiation, and a close consideration of the physical spaces wherein innovation unfolds. Collaboration and co-creation, which allow participants to work together and draw inspiration from what others are doing, are two additional core principles. Next, visual thinking, or communicating visually and inclusively, is yet another core principle of Design-Driven Innovation that helps people to gain a shared understanding of the problem and ideas. Visual thinking involves the use of physical artefacts that participants can use to establish a sustained emotional connection with the process. Activities like building prototypes can also improve decision-making by concretising abstract concepts. Learning in the context of Design-Driven Innovation is captured in its interface with the agile and lean start-up principles. These principles promote constant iteration to detect errors early, avoid risk, and for users to build confidence in their ideas (Dobrigkeit, de Paula, & Uflacker, 2019; Zorzetti et al., 2020).

Most of the approaches that underpin Design-Driven Innovation set the groundwork for being effectively used while developing new services and policies in cities, focussing on co-creation as the most useful tool for collaboration and the creation of innovations not only at a technological, but mostly at a socio-economic level.

3.2. GUIDING PRINCIPLES: 6C FRAMEWORK

Having examined three leading practice-oriented design frameworks that promote innovation through co-creation, we can now introduce six design principles for co-creation, which we call the *6C Framework* and which is present in Fig. 1.

The first C: *Co-creation is citizen-centred.* Rapid improvements in information communication technologies present cities with an important opportunity to improve services and achieve more with less. However, cities cannot take advantage of this opportunity if their citizens cannot and will not participate in the development and implementation of these technologies. By involving citizens, hidden and yet unmet needs may be revealed. What is more, through their experiences and knowledge, good ideas may come to the fore given the supportive and open environment (cf. Veeckman & van der Graaf, 2015). Involving citizens can improve services, lead to a more optimal use of public resources, and increase trust in the process and in government. At the same time, co-creation allows citizens to feel more competent and empowers them to actively participate in all walks of public life.

The second C: *Co-creation is collaborative.* Collaboration in co-creation unfolds across a complex network of relationships that binds together participants representing a broad range of interests. These ecosystems provide a rich environment for innovation and creativity that can leverage and build on specialised knowledge from these different sectors (Cox, Green, Borodako, & Sangiorgi, 2015). The formation and sustainability of such an ecosystem increases when all partners involved can draw value from co-creation (Veeckman et al., 2013). Collaboration is better when there are facilitative leaders who can encourage creativity, experimentation, and tolerance of unconventional solutions to prevailing problems faced by PSOs

(Brenner et al., 2016). Leadership and vision are needed so that such novel and yet untested ideas are nurtured and not prematurely crushed. Facilitative leadership that helps to detect and resolve potential conflicts, finds ways to encourage positive interactions, and helps identify yet unmet needs of various participants can to make collaborative processes more productive while ensuring the sustainability of the value which is generated (Bryson, Quick, Slotterback, & Crosby, 2013; Bussu & Bartels, 2014). Through such facilitative leadership, co-creation can generate collective intelligence.

The third C: *Co-creation is collective capital* (intelligence). The networked nature of co-creation is amplified by advances in ICTs, which enable the rapid sharing and agglomeration of date, information, and knowledge of all kinds and in different media formats (e.g., voice, video, text). In this new data-rich environment, learning must become a collective enterprise (Levy, 2015), wherein participants learn not only by gathering new knowledge but also through the experience of interacting with others. Learning in this collective environment must make good use of mistakes. 'Fail often and early' captures the idea that learning is enabled by experimentation and the open sharing of experiences with failures and mistakes (Brenner et al., 2016). This relates to the idea that value co-creation is an iterative process wherein evidence and experiences from previous experiments help inform thinking on a service and its design.

The fourth C: *Co-creation is creative*. Creativity arises from the opportunity for learning that connectivity enables. When citizens participate, their actions are expressions of creativity whereby they deploy and navigate the different norms, rules, and strategies in play within the process. In order to produce creative work, the componential theory of creativity sees three within-individual components that need to be in place (Amabile, 2011). First is the expertise of the individual, or the in-depth or in-breadth knowledge that someone brings into the process. Secondly, creativity-relevant processes need to be triggered, such as imaginative and flexible thinking. Last, there is task motivation. This latter point refers to the intrinsic motivations of participants (cf. Chapter 4), like a passion or profound interest in the theme. These three components are crucial for stimulating creativity and innovation, and which have to be supported throughout the co-creative processes. Ideally, creativity will be highest among (1) intrinsically motivated and (2) creative individuals (3) with high domain expertise and/or societal challenges.

The fifth C: *Co-creation considers context*. The city is the context in which co-creation takes place. A city is a place where people live, work, and play, and co-creation should be examined and designed in this real-life context. This context is multi-scalar, it is at the scale of the user, their group or community, the industry where they work, the city and the region, and co-creation must operate across this environment. In terms of community, a user can simultaneously belong to many communities, including 'communities of interest' to 'communities of practice' (Wenger, 1998). Belonging in a community provides a strong motivation to participate, to act collectively, and to keep participating in co-creation. The context includes the built environment, and the technical infrastructure that is necessary for users to participate in co-creation.

The sixth C: *Co-creation is culture*. Co-creation critically relies on shared norms and culture, and a willingness to learn and adapt. Openness, transparency, and value orientation are important for encouraging sustained participation by all stakeholders, particularly citizen users. A culture built around values provides all stakeholders with a shared sense of purpose which can sustain co-creation through challenging times. Openness is a core value of a co-creating culture, as diversity in views is a key innovation driver (Redlich et al., 2014). Openness is affected not just by who is participating but also by the values underpinning a culture. Instead, transparency is a key to promoting trusting relationships and to motivate participation in co-creation. Transparency can be achieved by being open about information which can be perceived negatively, like information about mistakes and errors. Generally, a sharing and innovative culture is upheld by values like equity, justice, and fairness. In a culture where these values resonate, they become a part of the design process itself.

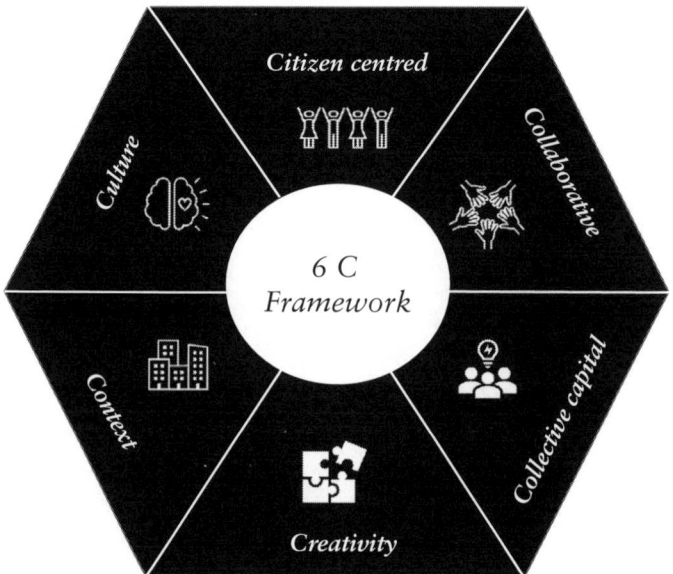

Fig. 1.   Co-Creation 6C Framework.

Taken together, these principles can be used to guide co-creation processes which avoid common pitfalls of participatory and interdisciplinary governance processes. When used in tandem with carefully selected and curated tools, they increase the likelihood that co-creation will be innovative, sustainable, and uphold core democratic values while generating public and individual values.

NOTE

1. See https://european-iot-pilots.eu/u4iot/toolkit/ (User Engagement for Large Scale Pilots in the Internet of Things (U4IoT), which received co-funding from the European Union's Horizon 2020 research and innovation programme under grant agreement no 732078 (2017–2019).

Chapter 4

TOOLS AND METHODS FOR VALUE CO-CREATION

Value co-creation with stakeholders can be demanding and challenging, but also very rewarding if done properly. Researchers around the world have worked extensively to develop design principles that can support stakeholder participation at all stages of the co-creation process (cf. Chapter 3). While manifold theories attempt to offer a comprehensive framework for better understanding what co-creation is and why it should be applied in cities, current knowledge of how to translate these frameworks into practice remains scant (cf. Chapter 5).

Therefore, this chapter presents a concise and clear roadmap for implementing co-creation in cities that follows a series of specific phases and sub-activities to whose several potential tools to be applied are mentioned. In this roadmap, co-creation stages are presented and unpacked. The roadmap or co-creation flowchart guides co-creators across these various stages spanning from exploration to dissemination. Then, tools are presented that can facilitate co-creation within these different stages with a number of practical illustrations. Numerous tools are available for co-creation, but their efficacy can vary according to the context in which co-creation will unfold. Out of this extensive set of tools, we selected some of the most innovative and proven to be successful in a city context.

This chapter offers thus a practical intermezzo, bridging theory and practice, and aims to guide public service organisations (PSOs) from the conventional to the experimental. A specific flowchart is offered, based on the 6C Framework (cf. Chapter 3) and on practical insights (cf. Chapter 5), to kick-off value co-creation with and by PSOs. The methods and tools described in this chapter aim to provide opportunities to structure conversations with stakeholders and to better understand their needs, with the ultimate aim to build more meaningful services or products.

4.1. CO-CREATION FLOWCHART

In this section, we lay out a flowchart template that practitioners can use to design their own co-creation project. Flowcharts are a handy visualisation tool for planning a co-creation process. They serve as an entry point for practitioners and enable to keep the bigger picture in mind. We list and detail the different phases and sub-activities of the co-creation process. Additionally, we review some of the most effective co-creation tools that can be implemented in the course of these activities. Practitioners are therefore able to select the tools that they find the most suitable to their own project and resources.

Our flowchart builds on main research paradigms from Chapter 3, namely Service Design, Living Labs and Design Thinking. Various PSOs, institutions and research centres have each adopted their own specific methodology to implement co-creation based on these theories and paradigms. We list a few of the most studied ones in order to construct a comprehensive flowchart and to provide additional inspiration to the reader.

The British Council's Double Diamond model has four distinct phases: discover, define, develop and deliver (Hambeukers, 2019). In its first phase, the central activities are gathering inspiration, insights, identifying user needs and developing initial ideas. The second and third phases focus on definition and prioritisation, followed by a period of development. The final phase focusses on the final testing, approval, launch and evaluation loops. Furthermore, the British Columbia Government specifically proposed a model in their Service Design Playbook to ensure public service design for British Columbians, although applicable to other governments (British Columbia, n.d.). Their methodology consists of six phases: alignment, discovery, opportunity, prototype & test, roadmap and implement. Another specific example is the Design Kit[1] of IDEO.org, which clusters methods and tools in three distinct phases: inspiration, ideation and implementation. Further specific toolkits which can be explored are the Service Design toolkit[2] from Namahn and Flanders DC, the Service Manual[3] for governmental departments in the UK, the DigitalGov's User Experience Program,[4] etc. For a complete overview of different toolkits, one can consult the database of The Observatory for Public Sector Innovation,[5] and use the filtering options for type of practice or discipline.

Next, Design Thinking proposes methodologies which heavily rely on multidisciplinary teams and on feedback loops with users. Service Design has its roots in Design Thinking and many have adopted the principles in their frameworks (e.g., the IDEO toolkit and the British Design Council). A specific Design Thinking process is outlined by The Hasso-Plattner Institute of Design at Stanford.[6] According to the school, they propose five stages of design thinking: empathise, define the problem, ideate, prototype and test. In the first stage, information is gathered to gain insight into users and their needs, for example, by immersing yourself in the physical environment of a prospective user. The second stage is related to synthesis and definition of a problem statement, which starts the preparations for the third stage by helping to look for ideas for solutions. In the ideation phase, the design team starts thinking outside of the box and will use methods and tools, such as brainstorming and brainwriting. In the final two stages, the prototype is tested, and the complete product will only be released after refinements and alterations. Other practical examples of using Design Thinking in Government can be found via The Design Thinking Foundation,[7] the handbook on Design Thinking for Public Excellence,[8] the Design Council in the UK,[9] and so forth.

In Living Lab ecosystems, we also see that based on experiences, various phases are proposed to guide the innovation process. Here, the proposed methodologies largely coincide with the natural stages of a product development process, with a specific focus on adding the perspective of user-driven and open innovation. As illustration, Steen and van Bueren (2017) discovered five different phases in (urban) Living Labs: research, development, testing, implementation, and commercialisation. The first phase focusses on the revision of the current state in order to reach understanding on the subject under investigation. The following stages, similar to Service Design, focus on the process of creating, growing and implementing a new product or service. Finally, the last stage is different from service design, and focusses specifically on marketing and commercialisation aspects of the product or service. Another example is the proposed methodology by the U4IoT project, which describes a methodological framework that follows design reasoning with three distinct phases: exploration, experimentation and evaluation (Malmberg et al., 2017). These phases include a quasi-experimental approach, with a pre-measurement, an intervention, and a post-measurement. Other examples of often used Living Lab methodologies are the FormIT methodology[10] proposed by the Botnia Living Lab and UnaLab,[11] and other frameworks provided in Schaffers, García Guzmán, and Merz (2010), Almirall, Lee, and Wareham (2012), Vicini, Bellini, and Sanna (2012) and Hossain, Leminen, and Westerlund (2019).

Last, the framework proposed by Ansell and Torfing (2021) is also worth mentioning, as they constructed an analytical framework by studying processes of co-creation. Their framework draws on network analysis, design theory and other relevant contributions and consists of four different phases: initiation, design, implementation and consolidation. The focus of the first phase is on the description of the problem that calls for a co-created solution, as well as identifying potential actors and motivating them to participate – with notions of building trust and collaboration. The second phase includes the redefinition of the problem while designing tentative solutions, and experimenting with the most promising one. The third phase and fourth phase focus on the launch of the solution and enfold activities as mobilising resources, routinising new behaviours, interconnection and coordination, dealing with opposition, etc. The final phase is about consolidation, upscaling and diffusion. In contrast to other particular frameworks, more attention is paid here to activities that help with the implementation of the solution, by focussing on new rules, procedures and patterns of behaviours that need to be adjusted.

From these and our own experiences, and taking into account the 6C Framework, the following main phases are included in our proposed flowchart:

• **Phase 1: Exploration** – This phase focusses on the scoping and the definition of the problem, the stakeholder mapping and problem verification.

• **Phase 2: Ideation** – This phase focusses on idea generation, selection and refinement.

• **Phase 3: Implementation** – This phase focusses on experimentation, with prototyping, testing and evaluation.

• **Phase 4: Diffusion** – The final phase focusses on dissemination of results, with the launch of the final product or service and upscaling activities.

A simplified draft visualisation of how we imagine the flowchart is presented in Fig. 2. The model should be visualised as an agile, circular model open to continuous iteration to avoid making mistakes in the process.

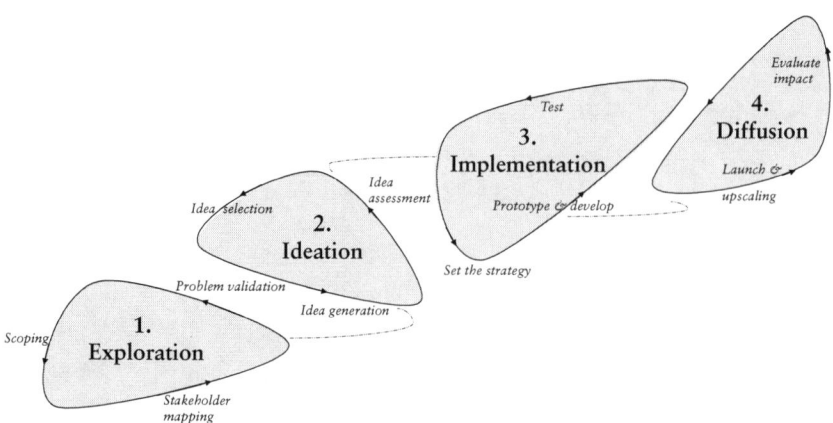

Fig. 2.   Co-creation Flowchart Design.

We recommend that practitioners apply this flowchart in an iterative manner and do not to rush through the steps. Co-creation projects have reported that longer phases would improve communication (especially in the first phases), increase participation and offer a better understanding of the why's and how's of the success of the different co-creation activities (Temmerman, Veeckman, & Ballon, 2021). In the following paragraphs, the different phases and their sub-activities are explained through various illustrations.

4.1.1. Phase 1: Exploration

Co-creation projects are not one-off meetings: they require enduring interactions and often develop through several iterations (Ansell & Torfing, 2021). Therefore, it is important to start co-creation projects with a thorough exploration phase that lays down a strong foundation for the rest of the process. In this sense, the exploration phase is of uttermost importance and should entail several activities: (1) a definition of the scope of the project through an initial problematisation; (2) a mapping of stakeholders that relate to the problem; and (3) a problem validation with a need's identification with the stakeholders.

Activity 1: Scoping and Initial Problematisation

Setting the objective and the goals of the co-creation initiative is the starting point of any co-creation strategy. Generally speaking, the problematisation emerges from a gap, a need that is not being met (Mulgan, 2006), or an initial impetus that can be external or internal to the initial group of actors involved (Neumeier, 2017). The initiator of a co-creation project is usually a public actor, and although it is not impossible for social entrepreneurs, civil society organisations or private firms to be initiators, public organisations are generally the ones to initiate the process as they have the resources, the capacities, and also the legitimacy and the authority to do so (Ansell & Torfing, 2021).

Depending on the initiator of the project, this activity can take various forms and is different from project to project. However, the goal is always the same: identify and characterise the problem, need or demand that has to be solved. To this end, several tools can be of great help when identifying and scoping the challenges for the co-creation strategy. Within this activity, we selected the following good practices, methods and tools: The Problem Canvas,[12] Brainwriting[13] (Litcanu, Prostean, Oros, & Mnerie, 2015), The Strategy Map (Kaplan, Norton, & Inc Books24x7, 2004), Frame your Design Challenge,[14] Duncker Diagram[15] (imagining the present and the desired state), etc. Furthermore, secondary research tools could be beneficial to have context and history. Therefore, classic research methods can be used, such as state-of-the-art reviews, expert interviews, surveys, etc. Notably, these tools are not mutually exclusive and can all be conducted within the same project, in any order that would make the most sense for the project.

THE PROBLEM STATEMENT IN THE 'AMAI! PROJECT'

The 'amai' project (literally: 'WOW'), funded by the Flemish Government (Department of Economics and Innovation) launched a citizen participation project in 2021 for identifying ideas and challenges around artificial intelligence. The main objective of the project is to raise awareness about the opportunities of artificial intelligence and to co-create innovative ideas in the domain of mobility, health, climate and work. During the initial exploration phase, several ideas and problems were identified through a citizen platform and workshops with the help of a problem statement canvas. The participants were requested to describe the context of the problem, the gainers and 'losers' of the challenge, the present versus the current state, the needed technological solutions and alternative shortcomings. These problem statements were used as input for launching a call-to-action and building of consortia to realise the identified challenges.

Activity 2: Stakeholder Mapping

To better understand the problem and how to solve it adequately, it is crucial to identify the stakeholders. On a daily basis, PSOs interact with a multitude of stakeholders and during service innovation processes, it is crucial to involve them in a meaningful way. In the broadest sense, stakeholder engagement can be defined as 'the process by which an organisation involves people who may be affected by the decision it makes or can influence the implementation of its decisions' (Stephens & Martin, 2019, p. 176). During the co-creation process, stakeholders can suppose or oppose certain design decisions, hold relevant positions or be affected with the outcomes in the long term. In this sense, a distinction should be made between end-users and stakeholders, as these are two different concepts. An end-user is the person who ultimately uses the end product or service and for whom the product of service is developed. On the other hand, a stakeholder is a group of individuals who is affected by the overall objectives, decision or activities from the co-creation process. However, depending on the situation, some people or organisations can act both as an end-user and as a stakeholder (Freeman, 2010). Stakeholders can be described according to their interactions within a knowledge economy, such as in the quadruple and quintuple innovation helix frameworks (Etzkowitz & Leydesdorff, 2000). In this framework, stakeholders are classified into university, industry, government, the public and the environment. However, one could also opt to classify their stakeholders according to their level of interest and influence each stakeholder has (Murray-Webster & Simon, 2006)

Depending on the project, the identification can result in one or several stakeholder groups: for example, if the problem identified in activity 1 is related to road safety for cyclists in the city, the primary target group would be 'cyclists of the city', but a secondary target group could be 'motorists in the city' and even 'truck drivers in the city' along with 'public transport drivers in the city', starting from the principle that it takes more than cyclists to create an accident.

After the identification, it is important to understand the target groups and characterise them on several elements that are relevant to the problem being investigated, such as socio-demographics, specific accessibility issues or motivation to participate. Taking the example of the cyclists, it could be said that they are generally aged 18–40 years old, male, that they mainly cycle to go to work – hence during day time – and that they generally do not wear reflective clothing. Profiling the target group is important, because it offers a first window of understanding into their daily life. Visualising and understanding the target group helps not only top-level management, but especially the actors who will have to implement the co-creation strategy with citizens. As such, they can familiarise themselves with their final users for producing effective results and impacts in the targeted communities. Second, it allows to determine how to best involve them in the project, as different target groups will call for different engagement protocols, type of co-creation activities or style of language used to interact with them (Tweddle, Robinson, Pocock, & Roy, 2012).

For this activity, the following methods and tools can be used: stakeholder mapping, personas (Pruitt & Adlin, 2006), panel circle (Malmberg et al., 2017), recruiting tools,[16] actors map[17] and so forth.

PANEL MANAGEMENT – USAGE OF THE PANEL CIRCLE BY IMEC.LIVING LABS

The imec.Living Labs organisation helps to recruit and engage end-users in open innovation projects, initiated by public or private stakeholders. In order to find the right profiles, with demanded skills and interest, they apply a two-step approach. First, they map all the different stakeholders needed in the living lab project, next, they organise the target groups in a circle. These groups positioned in the middle of the circle will be more actively involved than the groups out of the centre of the panel circle.

Activity 3: Problem Validation

The problems identified in activity 1 are often qualified as 'wicked challenges' in the sense that it is almost impossible for a single actor to come up with an adequate solution (Baccarne, Logghe, Schuurman, & De Marez, 2016). Such challenges often require negotiations between several actors to be solved (Mulgan, Tucker, Ali, & Sanders, 2007). Starting from the assumption that the affected and relevant groups are competent interpreters of their own lives (Mulgan, 2006), a validation of the problem identified in activity 1 as well as its specific characteristics is opportune to conduct, to make sure that the problematisation depicts an appropriate picture of the investigated issue. In this activity, participants redefine, purify or add elements to the pre-identified issues (Laenens, Mariën, & Walravens, 2019). This step is crucial if the goal is to truly bridge a gap and answer the needs of the target group. Likewise, this activity is of specific importance if the project is to be truly 'bottom-up' and driven from issues on the ground rather than political agendas.

The set of tools we suggest the cities to implement within this activity are: Value Proposition Canvas,[18] the lead users method,[19] needs assessments,[20] etc. Furthermore, classic research methods, such as (expert) interviews, focus groups and surveys can also work efficiently for validating the problem definition.

4.1.2. Phase 2 – Ideation

Once Phase 1 is completed and the problem and stakeholder network have been clearly identified, the creative part of the co-creation project can start. In this Ideation phase, the stakeholders will identify new ideas to face the pre-identified issue(s). In this phase, innovators play a central role, as they are often good at linking apparently unrelated methods and ideas together (Mulgan, 2006). However, ideas rarely emerge fully formed, and they will need to be assessed and re-worked to be suitable for the next phase 'Planning and experimentation'. During this stage, the usage of citizen participation platforms forms a great opportunity for collecting and evaluating ideas.

Activity 1: Idea Generation

The goal of this activity is to generate ideas on ways to deal with the identified problem (BEPA, 2010), with creativity as the main driver. Indeed, as the current situation has been identified as problematic in the first stage of the process, it is important to imagine new possibilities, or new ways to apply existing approaches of other domains to the problem area. As Mulgan (2006) notes, the key to success is to make sure that there is a range of choices as wide as possible to draw on. Latent needs and wants of end-users need to be discovered here, therefore, sensitising techniques are necessary.

The set of tools to implement in this activity is diverse and flourishing. To name a few, we recommend: open innovation hackathons (Baccarne et al., 2016), six thinking hats,[21] world café method (Slocum & Steyaert, 2003), co-creation workshops,[22] creative toolkits (Martin, Hanington, & Hanington, 2012), and so forth.

THE WORLD CAFÉ METHOD FOR CO-CREATING A CITIZEN SCIENCE GUIDEBOOK FOR PSOs

The World Café method is a participative method that was chosen to co-create a handbook on citizen science guidelines for PSOs. This handbook was the ultimate end goal of a one-year trajectory, which was financed by the Flemish Ministry for Internal Affairs, Civic Integration and Equal Opportunities (Belgium), in order to raise awareness of citizens science and spark interest in conducting citizen science experiments by and with PSOs. The World Café method is a creative process for facilitating a collaborative dialogue between participants and for promoting the sharing of knowledge and ideas during conversations. During a 3-month trajectory, approximately 18–20 participants, being representatives from major Flemish cities in Belgium, joined three sessions. In the sessions, groups were formed, and they debated on several major needs, barriers and opportunities of citizen science. After some time, the groups switched and built further on each other's information. In this way, there was a cross-pollination of the ideas generated over the different rounds. At the end of the process, the results are presented in a plenary session.

Activity 2: Idea Assessment and Selection

Once ideas have been formulated, the stakeholder network should proceed with an assessment to determine which solution to select. The assessment of ideas in terms of suitability and feasibility is of crucial importance. Mistakes at this step might generate issues in terms of acceptance of the solution by the stakeholder groups and end-users. For this reason, it is important for the target group to be involved in this process and contribute to the ingestion of ideas and analysis of their feasibility in real-life environments. In this activity, usually a user requirement analysis and prioritisation take place. The term refers to the activity of 'investigating and analysing an initial set of requirements that have been gathered, elicited or captured' (Kurniawan, 2004, p. 204). There are different types of requirements that can be investigated. First of all, one can focus on functional requirements. These requirements contain a description of what the system should do, or how the system should work. Next, there are the non-functional requirements: these requirements say what constraints there are on the system and its development, and refer to performance requirements of the system, such as security, logging, scalability, etc. Finally, there are data requirements: these requirements capture attributes about the required data on the platform, such as the type of data, volatility, size, amount, accuracy, etc. The set of requirements will be developed through an iterative process of negotiation, and will be the outcome of multiple data-gathering and interpretation activities. It is important that the identified requirements are justifiable and can be related back to the data, or the user needs that were collected. Performing a user requirements analysis is crucial to understand what the product under development should do, and to ensure that it supports the users' needs. If requirements are wrong, then the product could cause frustration, loss of confidence, lack of impact, etc.

The set of tools that cities can implement within this activity are storyboards,[23] assumption mapper,[24] tech cards (Ocnarescu et al., 2011), user requirement analysis (Kurniawan, 2004), scenario writing, etc.

THE PRIORITISATION OF USER REQUIREMENTS IN THE SAVINGFOOD PROJECT

In the SavingFood project, a food distribution platform was co-created by citizens, researchers and designers and representatives of food redistribution organisations. A user requirement analysis was set up in order to gather all the relevant requirements of the various stakeholders, such as community coordinators of farmer markets and gleaning activities, as well as from businesses with a food surplus. At the end of the user requirement gathering, the requirements were prioritised by the internal stakeholders of the project. They prioritised all the requirements on the level of importance for achieving the project's goal, the level of difficulty for technical implementation and the perceived user satisfaction. Prioritising the requirements was necessary to determine the relative necessity of each requirement, as some were more critical than others, and could improve the user satisfaction significantly. Furthermore, a balance had to be made between project realities of resources, timing and deadlines.

4.1.3. Phase 3: Implementation

Activity 1: Set the Strategy

Define action plans for achieving long-term impacts before developing the expected solution helps to increase the final benefits of the end result. At this stage, it is vital to build a plan that leverages from the inputs and insights of all relevant stakeholders especially for considering their needs, desires and requirements. The following activities, and in particular the testing of the end solution, will be more effective and easier to implement if a clear and shared co-creation strategy is envisioned together with the citizens even before the prototyping step. Be aware that strategic planning takes time and requires expertise and it is vital all stakeholders feel their opinion is valued in this process.

The set of tools to use during this activity are: tech cards (Ocnarescu et al., 2011), Ambition Setting, 5 Bold Steps Strategy[25] and so forth.

Activity 2: Prototype and Develop

The prototype phase is fundamental for testing the solution before initiating the final development process. The prototype is in fact a sample of the final product useful for validating a process or a solution with a restricted number of stakeholders. Usually within a city context, the prototypes are built directly with the citizens and ideally with a set of final users. The following activity, the development stage, aims to create a functional product out of the results from the testing of the prototype. Common product or process development mistakes include not generating enough prototypes, not allowing people to be involved in the process and use the solution in real life, as well as not planning accurately the next steps in the process, e.g., experimentation and evaluation of the impact produced by the product or process implemented in the targeted communities.

The most effective tools we suggest using during this activity are: storyboards (Martin et al., 2012), (paper) prototyping sessions with testing tasks (Snyder, 2003) or live prototyping,[26] A/B testing,[27] think-aloud protocols (Marsh, 2007), participant observations in the city (Martin et al., 2012), and so forth.

Activity 3: Test the Solution

User testing is usually applied in user-centred interaction design to validate a product together with the final stakeholders. The testing phase aims at evaluating the ability of the solution developed to meet the users' needs and their expectations. The testing phase is not just a process for gathering opinions or comments from a set of potential users but involves a clear set of systematic observations developed with the users in several iterations throughout the testing process.

There are several possible tools to be used within this approach. The tools we suggest during this phase are: Usability Testing; A/B testing,[28] Prototype Testing Map[29]; Blink testing,[30] participant observations in the city etc.

PARTICIPANT OBSERVATION IN THE CITY: SMART APPLICATIONS WITH ECIM

In the European Cloud Marketplace for Intelligent Mobility (ECIM) project, a smart parking application was co-created between end-users, designer teams and parking providers. To test the solution, users were requested to participate in a city game. This city game invited the participants to drive to a certain location, park their car and complete a questionnaire. In return, the participants received a free ticket for a visit to a museum. The participant observations made it possible to collect feedback on real-life situations and influence of context factors, such as for instance the connectivity in underground parking lots, the reaction speed, and other types of user experience issues, such as perceived ease of use and usefulness. Based on the user feedback, a second prototype was built that improved the functioning of the system significantly.

4.1.4. Phase 4: Diffusion

Activity 1: Launch and Upscaling of the Service or Product

After the implementation phase, the service or product should be in a mature enough state in order to launch it to the target audiences. Challenges can rise in this phase, such as the potential misalignment between new and existing solutions, the efforts required for learning how to use the new solution, and a potential organisational change if the new solution is introduced as part of the organisational culture (cf. Chapter 6). If the solution is satisfactory, the solution can be scaled up either by finding different target groups or by finding alternative needs. More people can benefit from the solution, or even new functionalities can be added so that the applicability is enhanced.

The set of tools during this activity are: networking, explore scalability,[31] sustainable revenue,[32] build partnerships[33] and keep iterating.[34]

Activity 2: Evaluate (Societal) Impact

The last activity of the co-creation process involves the evaluation of the outcomes and impacts generated by the whole approach at the end of the journey. The impact produced can be assessed at societal level, but it can also consider the economic and the technological impact. To perform such an evaluation assessment, the targeted stakeholders can be involved in the analysis of the results created, and this process can be implemented by taking into account both the short and long term. The evaluation helps to see if the actual problem statement is solved, and if the current state equals the desired state. Potential improvements can be identified to enhance the co-creation process.

The set of tools suggested during this activity are: I Like, I Wish, What If[35]; Dotmocracy[36] and the Monitor and Evaluate.[37]

EVALUATING OUTCOMES AND IMPACTS OF FAMILIES_SHARE THROUGH AN IMPACT ASSESSMENT METHODOLOGY

In the Families_Share project, a digital social innovation platform was co-designed in order to share time and tasks among families for organising informal childcare. After the co-creation journey, with seven pilot experiments in several European countries (Belgium, Italy, Greece and Hungary), the solution was evaluated with both internal and external project stakeholders to assess its socio-economic outcomes and impacts. Several indicators were chosen, such as parent and child wellbeing, social capital, user empowerment, economic benefit, etc., to iteratively evaluate the impact of the solution. Specific barriers and enablers were also explored in order to ameliorate the adoption of the solution among public authorities. The results helped to ameliorate and further define the sustainability plans of the seven pilots. More information: https://www.families-share-toolkit.eu/

NOTES

1. https://www.designkit.org/human-centered-design

2. https://servicedesigntoolkit.org/index.html

3. https://www.gov.uk/service-manual

4. https://www.usability.gov/how-to-and-tools/guidance/gsa-first-fridays-program. html

5. https://oecd-opsi.org/search-toolkits/?_sft_discipline-or-practice=service-design

6. https://dschool.stanford.edu/resources/getting-started-with-design-thinking

7. https://www.design-thinking-association.org/explore-design-thinking-topics/ vertical-markets/design-thinking-in-government

8. https://www.undp.org/content/dam/undp/library/capacity-development/English/ Singapore%20Centre/GPCSE_Design%20Thinking.pdf

9. https://www.designcouncil.org.uk/design-public-sector

10. https://www.ltu.se/cms_fs/1.101555!/file/LivingLabsMethodologyBook_ web.pdf

11. https://unalab.enoll.org/

12. https://www.metabeta.com/articles/process/problem-statement-canvas/

13. https://unalab.enoll.org/brainwriting/

14. https://www.designkit.org/methods/frame-your-design-challenge

15. http://umich.edu/~scps/html/05chap/frames_prof.htm

16. https://www.designkit.org/methods/recruiting-tools

17. https://unalab.enoll.org/the-actors-map/

18. https://unalab.enoll.org/value-proposition-canvas/

19. https://www.lead-innovation.com/english-blog/how-to-develop-innovations-with-the-lead-user-method

20. https://www.lead-innovation.com/english-blog/how-to-develop-innovations-with-the-lead-user-method

21. https://unalab.enoll.org/6-thinking-hats/

22. https://www.designkit.org/methods/co-creation-session

23. https://www.designkit.org/methods/co-creation-session

24. https://unalab.enoll.org/assumption-mapper/

25. https://unalab.eu/en/node/238

26. https://www.designkit.org/methods/live-prototyping

27. https://unalab.enoll.org/a-b-testing/

28. https://unalab.enoll.org/a-b-testing/

29. https://unalab.enoll.org/prototype-testing-map/

30. https://unalab.enoll.org/prototype-testing-map/

31. https://www.designkit.org/methods/explore-scalability

32. https://www.designkit.org/methods/sustainable-revenue

33. https://www.designkit.org/methods/build-partnerships

34. https://www.designkit.org/methods/keep-iterating

35. https://unalab.enoll.org/i-like-i-wish-what-if/

36. https://unalab.enoll.org/dotmocracy/

37. https://www.designkit.org/methods/monitor-and-evaluate

Chapter 5

CO-CREATION IN CITIES: A SET OF TESTIMONIALS

Co-creation in the public sector is applied as a new mode of public service management that aims to better address societal needs and challenges, which are increasingly fragmented in modern society (Bason, 2010). Using this reform strategy, public services are built on the principles of democratic citizenship, organisational humanism, and social innovation (Denhardt & Denhardt, 2000). Through a variety of co-creation methods and tools, such as experimental Living Labs or citizen juries, co-creation is becoming inherently part of the public sector's toolbox (cf. Chapters 3 and 4). Co-creation enables citizens to share feedback and to, at the same time, extract value for their own good. Citizens' participation in these co-creative processes emphasises innovation and creativity, but also implies a fundamental change regarding the roles, positions, and relationships between stakeholders (Leino & Puumala, 2020). With the interest in the co-creation premise, the organisational model breaks free from a closed, hierarchically organised, and top-down model to transition into an open model which relies on bottom-up engagement and multi-stakeholder collaboration. Public service innovations will only produce outcomes that matter when key stakeholders are actively involved in a design process, supported by multidirectional communication and learning (Agusti et al., 2014). Co-creation thus requests a shift not only in the organisational culture (cf. Chapter 6), but also in mentality. Co-created knowledge can only be impactful when it is turned into concrete action by and integrated in decision-making processes of the city administration.

New technologies have also enabled citizens to co-create in a digital way with their local government (Agusti et al., 2014). Digital technologies can empower individuals and increase the opportunities for more person-alised and demand-driven public services (Meijer, 2012; Noveck, 2015). Lember et al. distinguish sensing, communication, processing and actuation technologies that each have their respective positive and negative impacts on co-creation (Lember, Brandsen, & Tõnurist, 2019). For instance, through sensing technologies, citizens can collect and monitor environmental data in their city about the traffic, water or air quality. As such, technologies give citizens the opportunity to collect insights and deliberate with government representatives on local policies. Moreover, it can lead towards a data-driven co-creation, whereby citizens as 'explorers' can help to identify, discover and define problems in public services (Nambisan & Nambisan, 2013). However, technology may also be a barrier for participation or hamper equal participa-tion. It should be ensured that all voices are still heard and that local govern-ments are not drowned in a data overload.

This chapter focusses on opportunities and challenges of co-creation in the public sector through a set of testimonials and a literature-informed analysis. Why do local city governments decide to co-create with citizens, and which barriers may hamper the adoption of co-creation? The gains of co-creation seem obvious, however, translating the potential of co-creation into practice seems more challenging. A set of testimonials present lessons learned of co-creating with citizens for public service management. As such, the chapter provides some key learning points that can be extracted from past and current examples in Europe.

5.1. OPPORTUNITIES OF CO-CREATION

Co-creation for Public-Sector Innovation

Public-sector innovation is defined as 'new ideas that work at creating public value' and which result in better public results including efficiency, effectiveness, satisfaction and quality (Daglio, Gerson, & Kitchen, 2014, p. 4). By innovating public services, city governments can increase the responsiveness of services to local needs and to keep up with public expectations. Innovation is a core activity for constraining cost pressures and to guarantee a smooth operation (Mulgan & Albury, 2003). An innovation ecosystem and an innovation platform critically support co-creation in the public sector with citizens (Nambisan & Nambisan, 2013). Looking at the innovation systems in the public sector, there are various perspectives and traditions, such as open innovation (Chesbrough, 2003), user-driven innovation (von Hippel, 2005), triple helix models (Etzkowitz & Leydesdorff, 2000), and more recently networked governance (Hartley, 2005), community governance (Hess & Adams, 2007) and collaborative innovation with the central notion of co-creation (Bason, 2010). These different systems stress that innovation does not occur in isolation, but depends upon the interplay between different stakeholders among whom knowledge is shared and recombined (Bloch & Bugge, 2013). This ecosystem, with a community of innovators, promotes a shared perspective on the problem-solving process and defines the architecture of participation (Nambisan & Nambisan, 2013). Ideally, the innovation ecosystem is supported by an innovation platform, either physical or virtual, which provides a venue for citizen co-creation. Through this platform, the problem-solving process and the knowledge exchange is supported. It allows participants to share problem-related data and knowledge, and provides fitted communication protocols for actors to interact with one another (Nambisan & Nambisan, 2013).

Citizens' engagement in public service innovation can increase the efficiency and effectiveness of the city government at different levels. First, the services can be better fitted to the users' needs and expectations (Toots, McBride, Kalvet, & Krimmer, 2017), especially when dealing with multiple requests from different stakeholders (Alves, 2013). Furthermore, co-creation can yield services which are more holistic and synergistic than existing solutions, or in new solutions that even outperform the previous ones (Sørensen & Torfing, 2011). Thirdly, through co-creation, the city government can tap into the resources of citizens themselves (Agusti et al., 2014). With the help of digital technologies, citizens can collect real-time data and send it directly to their city administration. As such, the city government can rely and build on the collective input of citizens to enact policy. Furthermore, co-creating public services can improve the allocation of resources especially when public administrations lack the ideas, means or resources to solve wicked problems all by themselves (Warren, 2009). Last, the value of co-creation can also be found in experimental learning through pilot demonstration projects. In these innovation projects, actors engage in the processes of trial and error, which help to reduce the costs of initial failures and enable fast learning and adaptation (Ansell & Torfing, 2021). The city of Issy-les-Moulineaux, for instance, shows how pilot studies helped them launch an open data portal and deliver an interactive dashboard on mobility. Co-creation was applied for testing and evaluating the solutions and gave the City Council the certainty on the technology's usefulness and user-friendliness.

ISSY-LES-MOULINEAUX: LAUNCHING AN OPEN DATA PORTAL THROUGH LEARNING-BY-DOING

Since 2012, the city of Issy-les-Moulineaux has been pursuing an active open data policy. The data.issy.com portal is a result of many efforts that were supported by experimental learning studies in several European-funded projects, such as Citadel...On the move, Open Transport Net and PoliVisu. The city opted for a long-term strategy with the co-creation of different open data interfaces for diverse target groups. Experimental learning with users helped Issy-les-Moulineaux to collect experiences, to better understand users' needs and to discover how to proceed in the future with their open data policy. Matteo Satta, EU Project Manager at the city of Issy-les-Moulineaux testifies that 'Co-creation gives the opportunity to test an innovation. Even if an innovation is not so good, it is a lesson learned. You test something to have an answer, the problem occurs when you do not find the answer on how to do it. In this sense, the pilot studies gave us a certainty for adoption and a platform fit for use'.

These projects left a legacy that deserved to be emulated. In 2019, the city launched a dashboard that visualises real-time transport data, and which is the sum of all lessons learned. The dashboard received a prize as part of the 4th Open Data Trophies by OpenData France and La Gazette. The dashboard was realised in collaboration with OpenDataSoft and Datactivists.

Interview with Matteo Satta, City of Issy-les-Moulineaux,
EU Project Manager

Co-creation for Democratisation

Besides innovation-related benefits, co-creation can also have a democratising effect (Torfing et al., 2019). By changing the way governments engage with citizens in public service innovation, co-creation can provide an effective approach for fostering an open, transparent, and more deliberative public administration. In classical public bureaucracy, citizens are seen as mere passive actors and are placed on the receiving end of public services (Tribe, 2019). As a consequence, public service management is too narrowly focussed on efficiency and public regulation, and promotes asymmetric power relations between citizens and public authorities (Niskanen, 1971). Instead, co-created public governance brings central features of participatory and deliberative democracy into innovation systems (Lund, 2018). Participatory democracy is a model of democracy which provides actual decision-making power to citizens. The methodology emerged in the 1960s, but weakened and revived in the 2000s with the notion of participatory citizenship (Leino & Puumala, 2020; Noveck, 2015). This form of democracy claims that 'political decisions should be the product of fair and reasonable discussion and debate among citizens' (Eagan, 2017, retrieved from Encyclopedia Britannica). Co-creation has the promise of creating an interactive democracy, which is both participatory and deliberative (Neblo, Esterling, & Lazer, 2018). In this interactive democracy, political solutions are designed for and by citizens, but also with the citizens (Rosanvallon, 2011). Sørensen and Bentzen define interactive democracy as 'a form of representative democracy in which elected politicians make authoritative political decisions after having engaged in close dialogue with relevant and affected citizens' (2020, p. 140). Citizens are thus invited to collaborate with public actors in defining citizens the challenges, designing the solutions and implementing them in practice. This is often aided by modern information technology, which enables more interactive decision-making processes (Brill, 2019).

Improved decision-making is one of the key democratising effects that can be realised through co-creation (Baptista, Alves, & Matos, 2020). Implementing co-creative processes can increase public input and equity in decision-making and help build consensus (Agusti et al., 2014). Therefore, citizens and other stakeholders must be involved from the outset of the decision-making process, starting with the identification of the problem. Co-creation can also deepen participation and help to (re)connect politicians with citizens (Ansell & Torfing, 2021). Especially for institutions that are perceived as being distant from citizens, co-creation can boost democratic legitimacy, accountability and transparency (Torfing et al., 2019). Furthermore, Ansell and Torfing (2021) see opportunities in co-creation for solving the political problem, which they describe as the inability to provide 'robust policy solutions to complex societal problems for political action' (p. 29). This mismatch between policies and today's challenges is caused by political and institutional factors, but also by the increased complexity of today's modern challenges. Ansell and Torfing (2011) see an opportunity in the provision of complementary evidence by citizens for policymaking, evaluation and generation of new policies. As such, one can ensure that the developed policies are within public interest and well-grounded in society (European Commission, Joint Research Centre, 2016). In this philosophy, the PoliVisu project, together with the city of Mechelen and the citizen science organisation 'Telraam', delivered a dashboard about the implementation of a school street in Mechelen-Nekkerspoel (Belgium). PoliVisu applied a citizen science approach to measure the impact on mobility and safety in the surrounding neighbourhoods. Through citizen science, or the active participation of citizens in the data collection and further research phases on impact measurement, they ensured the active dialogue between pupils and their parents, the school and citizens from the neighbourhood (Acar, Raes, Rosseau, & Satta, 2021).

EVIDENCE-BASED POLICYMAKING THROUGH CITIZEN SCIENCE: THE IMPACT OF TEMPORARY ROADBLOCKS FOR A SAFER SCHOOL ENVIRONMENT

In 2020, the PoliVisu project developed an interactive dashboard to visualise the impact of 'school streets'. A school street intends to reduce the traffic around schools, at the beginning and the end of a school day. The road is temporarily physically blocked to prevent all motorised traffic. Usually, this is unpopular among people living in the surrounding streets as there is a risk of increased motorised traffic. Therefore, the PoliVisu project, together with the city of Mechelen and Telraam organised interactive workshops with local stakeholders, including pupils and their parents, citizens from the neighbourhood, mobility and smart city experts and the alderman for mobility in Mechelen. During these sessions, the set-up of the school street was explained, as well as its usefulness and call-to-action for citizens to participate by collecting data by installing a sensor for traffic measurement. The measurement device was installed in the front window and counted the traffic. The collected counts were made available for policymaking and research, and to measure the impact of local mobility policies. The interactive process and dialogue among diverse stakeholders, together with the support of the local city administration, generated lessons on how to create ownership, support and engagement on the establishment of the school street: 'You can gather the knowledge of citizens and use it for policymaking. Someone can come up with a suggestion, of which no one else has thought of before and which can lead towards the ideal solution. Gathering this local knowledge can lead towards the inclusion of different perspectives, which can bring a totally different outcome'. As a result, the data was used for dialogue in the community and ensured that there was no negative impact perceived by people living in the neighbourhood (Acar et al., 2021).

Interview with Lieven Raes, Informatie Vlaanderen,
EU Project Manager

Co-creation for more Resilient Communities

The third category of opportunities of co-creation is symbolic and shows that co-creation can be a goal in itself.

First, co-creation can help in strengthening citizenship. The legal construction and definitions of citizenship have evolved over time, but broadly it 'encompasses the rights and opportunities people should be able to expect from the governance of their society as well as their obligations' (Public Policy and Democratic Citizenship, 2007, p. 1). Through co-creation, citizens can cultivate an active, political citizenship based on rights and obligations. Citizens can see themselves as 'makers' of public services (Ansell & Torfing, 2021), and help solve problems by mobilising resources and ideas that enhance their quality of life (Nabatchi et al., 2017). In this sense, co-creation hails citizens who have a moral obligation to consider how they can contribute to the creation of new solutions, which might be important for themselves, but also their community and towards the society as a whole (Ansell & Torfing, 2021). For instance, Leino et al. (2020b) showcase how citizenship flourished through the co-creative processes and, on top, strengthened the social cohesion. Citizens participate in deliberative policymaking processes because of their need to feel like a part of the community and a need to belong to their city (Leino & Puumala, 2020). Co-creation can thus help in redefining citizenship, both in its political and social dimensions. It brings citizens together and encourages bonding between them, as they all contribute to a common cause.

Next, co-creation can also strengthen social capital (Voorberg et al., 2015). Social capital, or the 'resources embedded in a social structure which are accessed and/or mobilized in purposive actions' (Dubos, 2017, p. 12), is also an accelerator to participate in co-creative processes. When social ties are strong, people are more willing to participate and share their resources for the community (Voorberg et al., 2015). Social capital can thus be both a prerequisite for effective co-creation, as well as an outcome of it. The social capital created by certain 'communities of practice', or 'groups of people who share a concern or a passion for something they do and learn how to do it better as they interact regularly' (Wenger, 2011, p. 1), can play a key factor in public service management. Communities of practices come together, exchange knowledge, and foster unexpected ideas and innovations. They often have a shared competence, interest in a specific domain, help each other, interact and learn together.

Furthermore, co-creation can also foster trust (Fledderus, 2018). Hereby, Fledderus identifies several factors in the three stages of service delivery, which might have an effect on the trust relation between citizens and public institutions. Amongst others, the sense of control, motivation and trust in fellow citizens significantly shape service innovation (Fledderus, 2018). In terms of the acceptance of governance processes, increasing the transparency of the functioning of government institutions can raise citizen awareness of the experienced difficulties. Transparency can show how difficult it can be to implement change, and in turn, it can help in managing expectations among citizens and policy makers (Leadbeater, 2004). In turn, this can help in promoting acceptance and respect of the governance process (Baka, 2017).

In sum, through supporting active citizenship, the building of social capital and trust, co-creation can lead towards the creation of more resilient communities (Torfing et al., 2019). Resilience stands for 'patterns of positive adaptation during or following significant adversity or risk' (Snyder & Lopez, 2009, p. 118). The meaning of resilience has been subject to debate, however, one can speak about resilience if (i) a positive adaptation and (ii) a context with exposure to a significant challenge or risk are present (Snyder & Lopez, 2009). Various studies signify the great potential of co-creation to improve the resilience of communities related to disaster management, or for instance COVID-19 more recently (cf. Davies, 2019; Rao, 2021). Furthermore, the establishment of resilient cities and communities is an aim of the 2030 Agenda for Sustainable Development, which attributes a significant role to local governments and the need for participatory approaches to address contemporary challenges (United Nations, n.d.). In this regard, various communities of practices in Brussels are nowadays debating how local air quality can strengthen urban resilience. The Government of the Brussels Capital Region was ordered by court in January 2021 to take up additional actions in its air pollution monitoring policy, which is putting residents' health at risk (Guillot & Schaart, 2021). The local initiative, 'Luchtpijp' (air pipe), initiated by Beweging.net and Christelijke Mutaliteit (Christian health insurance fund), distributes air quality measurement kits to citizens. They aim to raise awareness on the topic, stimulate a debate on health issues, and make more profound conclusions on how good or bad the local air quality is. The volunteer, Rik Drabs, is a leading community member who helped to install public displays that inform citizens about the local air quality.

INCREASING RESILIENCE TO AIR POLLUTION IN BRUSSELS: THE POWER OF CITIZEN VOLUNTEERS

Since 2018, the initiative 'Luchtpijp' has been distributing low-cost air quality kits to citizens in Brussels. The project was initiated out of a need for more information about the local air quality in Brussels, due to a lack of official measurement points and lack of information on potential health risks. The sensor data, of almost 1.000 sensors, is collected via a centralised website and gives a real-time indication of how good or bad the local air quality is. Rik Drabs, a citizen living in Brussels, volunteers at Luchtpijp. He used his engineering background to design a public display in summer 2020 to make passers-by aware of the local air quality: 'I wrote the code and developed the design of the display. It is a display for the public space to make people aware about the local air quality and alert them that the air is being monitored. It took me some time to develop it, but I love to do this'. The display is currently installed at a school gate in the commune Herent and informs pupils and their parents about the local air quality. Thanks to Rik's voluntary contributions, the passers-by now know in a glimpse the local air quality and the impact of their behaviours, such as the organisation of school streets.

Interview with Rik Drabs, Beweging.net, Citizen volunteer

5.2. CHALLENGES OF CO-CREATION

Co-creation and the Organisational Context in PSOs

The first challenge for the set-up of co-creative processes in and with public service organisations (PSOs) is related to its organisational context. PSOs are still discovering and experimenting with co-creation or have not used it so far. This causes either the organisational culture (cf. Chapter 6), and/or specific organisational structures and processes are not directly compatible with co-creation.

Organisational culture is defined by the organisations' employees' shared beliefs, values and practices (Edwards, 1988). The transition towards an organisation which works in an open and multi-directional way with external stakeholders for service innovation can demand a huge transformation (Toots et al., 2017). The organisational culture in PSOs can differ on valued principles and be classified into flexible and collaborative or stable and internal (Cameron & Quinn, 2011). From innovative business culture, we learn

that innovativeness stands for organisations that are proactive in exploring new opportunities (Menguc & Auh, 2006), favour external orientation,
value the customers as sources of innovation and with an outside-in process
in the innovation activity (Leticia Santos-Vijande, González-Mieres, & Ángel
López-Sánchez, 2013). However, public administrations often work in silos,
which maximise vertical coordination. The shortcomings of a silos-dominant
administrative culture include difficulty in sharing information and impedi-
ments to the progression from decision to action (Scott & Gong, 2021).
Without proper co-ordination mechanisms, each department of the organisation might provide different solutions for the same problem (Homburg
& Jensen, 2007), potentially causing a loss of time and misunderstandings
(Kotter, 2008). Furthermore, another organisational barrier to public-sector
co-creation is the extent to which an administrative culture is risk averse. Risk
is inherent in every industry and innovation process, and creating a culture of
risk taking and experimentation demands a journey of change (Husk, 2018).
In the context of PSOs, there is a particular political risk and public scrutiny. In the pursuit of avoiding criticism or failure, it demotivates employees
to share innovative ideas – as innovation is inherently risky (Commission,
Australian Public Service, 2018). Therefore, Tummers, Voorberg, and Bekkers
(2015) recommend that public officials are trained in risk management and
tolerance in co-creation initiatives.

In terms of organisational structures and processes, Toots et al. (2017)
observe that incompatible organisational processes are a major barrier to
data-driven service co-creation. They detect concrete issues like the resistance
of the public sector to change, insufficient trust, weak political will and inadequate resources (Toots et al., 2017). Relatedly, Rösler, Söll, Hancock, and
Friedli (2021) focussed on the necessary organisational capabilities of PSOs
to adopt public value co-creation. The organisational capabilities refer to the
organisations' abilities to deploy resources to perform a certain activity (Grant,
1999). These resources can be either tangible or intangible, like infrastructure,
information and communication technology (ICT)-equipment or knowledge,
skills and competencies. The specific identified capabilities for public value
co-creation were 'individuated empowerment', 'reciprocal knowledge development and building', 'foundational interaction', 'coordinated integration'
and 'communication' (Rösler et al., 2021). These capabilities are linked to
a team's collaborative success and also refer back to the cultural controls of
an organisation (Rehman, 2019). Another barrier is the inflexibility of one's
identity and role in co-creation. For instance, Torfing et al. (2019) observe that
public employees that strongly identify with the roles of professional 'reliev-
ers' and 'care providers', might experience difficulties when collaborating

and mobilising the resources of external stakeholders. In this latter role as an 'enabler', public administrations share the power through the processes of co-created policymaking. Hence, there might be a potential lack of willingness to change, because of fears of losing status and control (Toots et al., 2017).

Besides an organisational shift and innovation learning, PSOs might thus also require a shift in role perception in order to set foot in the co-creation arena. In this respect, the collaboration between the Municipality of Porto and the Porto Digital Association is a good example of such a transformative collaboration. The Porto Digital Association[1] is initiated by the Municipality of Porto, the University of Porto and the Portuguese Business Association in order to promote ICT projects.

FOSTERING AN INNOVATION MINDSET IN THE MUNICIPALITY OF PORTO: PORTO DIGITAL

The Porto Digital Association started in 2014 as an independent entity for developing innovation and a digital strategy in the Municipality of Porto. The association has a close collaboration with the University of Porto, which is crucial in their partnership: 'It allows them to develop projects with a research and development focus and to implement solutions that reach out the early adopters of the innovations' explains Paulo Calçada – CEO of Porto Digital. It focusses on both the hardware and software layers of innovation. Porto Digital has experience in deploying 'smart' technology in the city of Porto, such as a free Wi-Fi network and sensing technology. They also implement a software layer which focusses on methodologies and on catalysing ideas and challenges for fostering start-ups in the ecosystem. In this last software layer, services are developed for and with the citizens through co-creation.

Paulo Calçada: 'We started four years ago with this new layer of co-creation. Together with the Municipality of Porto we are using the Service Design methodology to develop innovations. We are supporting the teams of the Municipality of Porto in redesigning the services. However, at first, it was hard for the Municipality to implement these changes, as it requested an innovative mindset. We helped and taught them why they should invest.' The Municipality of Porto went through a journey of change, whereby they had to get used to investing extra time in thinking about the services. The tendency was to have the services and products as quickly as possible, but which often didn't succeed – resulting in a never-ending process of innovation. The teams of the municipality had to familiarise themselves with methods and approaches for rethinking, redesigning and prototyping: 'You spend more time in defining the service, but in the end you gain by deploying it – this requested a shift in the whole organization'.

The 'Explore Porto' application is a concrete result of co-creation with citizens, the municipalities' teams, external experts, companies and non-profit organisations for promoting alternative modes of public transport in Porto. Together, they created a mobile web application for citizens and visitors to explore the city in a different way. Around 1,000 signalling devices – blue dots/beacons – in the city provide real-time information about points-of-interest and mobility. The service promotes the usage of public transport towards citizens and helps tourists in promoting a diversification of tourism in the city. The application is very successful, with over 20,000 users and will also be implemented in other European cities, such as in Helsinki. The application can be accessed via https://explore.porto.pt/.

Paulo Calçada, Porto Digital, CEO

Co-creation and Inclusive Practices

Value co-creation can have a democratising effect on public service. It has the capacity to transform public-sector practices into a multi-directional approach and increase the legitimacy of decisions (Michels, 2011). Hence, co-creation can contribute to the inclusion of citizens in urban policy and governance (cf. Lund, 2018). However, the democratic quality of co-creation is also measured by its equality and inclusion. According to Quick and Feldman (2011, p. 272), inclusion practices can be defined as 'continuously creating a community involved in coproducing processes, policies, and programmes for defining and addressing public issues'. They apply a broadened view on inclusion, with practices focussing on capacity building, connections and interactions across issues, sectors and engagement efforts. This definition contrasts with the common use of the term by the scholars of democratic theory, which rather describe it as the diversity of participants. In this latter perspective, democratic inclusion refers to equal influence over debate and decision-making within a polity by all those who are affected (Young, 2002, p. 8). Young argues that this definition raises questions on who needs to be involved and how strongly. Coupled with the term of political equality, inclusion should allow the maximum expression of interest, opinions and perspective relevant to the issue (Young, 2002). Similarly, Leino and Puumala (2020) found that in co-creation, some citizens will have more time, energy and the resources than others to contribute. The question thus arises if co-creation might exclude certain profiles. Inadequate access or capabilities to participate, might thus result in a biased participation (Torfing et al., 2019) that favours (once, again) the most extreme and/or advantaged segments enabling them to disproportionately influence joint decisions and may ignore those who should be included in decision-making. In this sense, recommendations that minimise the risk of reinforcing existing inequalities are helpful. First, it is recommended that participant's previous knowledge and resources are considered (Leino & Puumala, 2020). Furthermore, equal access to participation should be provided to all and that even low-tech approaches are feasible (Agusti et al., 2014). Last, resource asymmetries can be compensated by empowering weaker actors and giving them a veto in final decisions (Ansell & Torfing, 2021).

In any case, the inclusion of all potential participants in a co-creation process is not feasible. A certain limit should be set, otherwise the process will become very demanding in terms of logistics, communication and leadership. As a consequence, some of the affected actors will be included, but also will also be excluded (Ansell & Torfing, 2021). In this perspective, Floridia (2017) argues that it is not necessary to include everyone as a person, as long as their viewpoints and arguments are represented in the mediation process.

ACCESSIBLE CO-CREATION TOOLS: DESIGN PROBES IN THE 'HACKABLE CITY' PROJECT

In the 'Hackable City' project, several lessons learned were collected on how to set up inclusive practices for co-creation. This research project aimed to explore how digital media platforms could be used for an open, democratic process of collaborative city making between diverse stakeholders. The project, running from 2014 till 2016, focussed on the specific district 'Buiksloterham' – a neighbourhood and brownfield redevelopment site in Amsterdam (The Netherlands). In Buiksloterham, a co-creative process was set up between scientists, architects, neighbourhood associations, citizens and also the city of Amsterdam. Together, they interacted about the redevelopment of the site and started to think about the circular management of resources.

During the process, design probes were used to stimulate debate on collaborative development among the stakeholders. The design probes, in the form of a city game and workshops, helped to open up the process of city making and imagine an ideal model of the 'hackable' city. Martijn de Waal, Professor at the Amsterdam University of Applied Sciences, explains that these design probes were inspired through a research by design approach and were used to collect insights about the nature of the problem, as well as the preferred state to be brought about. In every step of the design process, the accessibility and usability of the tools and results were reflected upon: 'We tried to make it as accessible as possible for the community, therefore, we stepped away from scientific discourse and opted for games or procedures which helped to tease responses'.

In terms of inclusive practices, he explains that the design probes helped to stimulate debate in a playful way and responded to social motivations: 'It helped the participants to express their concerns in a playful manner and to easily make new connections. Thanks to the design probes, there was a communal mission as the end goal.' Another lesson learned was to work with intermediary organisations: 'It might take up to several years in order to reach the right profiles, you need to constantly invest in network building'. Therefore, the university often works with an agency for social and sustainable innovation in order to reach out to vulnerable target groups in Amsterdam. Last, another lesson learned is to make the process not too time consuming and to provide a rightful intrinsic motivation to participate.

Martijn de Waal, Amsterdam University of Applied Science,
Professor at the New Media and Public Space Department

Stakeholder Engagement and Co-creation

The last identified challenge related to the set-up of co-creation is stakeholder engagement. On a daily basis, PSOs engage with a significant number of stakeholders. In the broadest sense, a stakeholder can be defined as 'a person such as an employee, customer, or citizen who is involved with an organization, society, etc. and therefore has responsibilities towards it and an interest in its success' (Cambridge Dictionaries Online, n.p.). Being successful in co-creation requires the identification and involvement of all potential categories of stakeholders in its entire process (cf. Chapter 3). In this regard, it is also crucial to involve internal stakeholders from the concerned governmental departments and to have good teamwork in the handling of the proposed ideas.

Setting up co-creation initiatives might thus not be so straightforward in practice. Behavioural barriers are barriers affecting the behaviours of stakeholders involved in co-creation (Baptista et al., 2020). These include risk aversion and resistance to change, lack of interest in participating, lack of experience, time, and emotional involvement in issues. The first set of barriers, related to risk aversion and resistance to change, were already discussed previously in the context of the development of an organisational culture in the public sector. The latter barriers deal with a lack of intrinsic motivation to participate and mostly situate on the user side (Toots et al., 2017). Other potential barriers might be personal characteristics and values, awareness of participation opportunities, participation skills, and the overall ease of participation (Toots et al., 2017). There should be a good mix in the type of stakeholders, a clear objective on what to achieve and how, and the necessary resources. In this respect, Mogstad, Høiseth, and Pettersen (2018) recommend creating ownership in a project in order to successfully engage stakeholders. Specifically, for internal stakeholders, they see three physiological needs that need to be satisfied, which is competence, autonomy and relatedness. On the other hand, for successful engagement of external stakeholders, it is recommended to work on socialisation with other users and other intrinsic motivations like stimulating curiosity and providing an environment for learning (Fernandes & Remelhe, 2016).

A VISION FOR PUBLIC VALUE CO-CREATION: THE DIFFERENCE BETWEEN PHILOSOPHY AND PRACTICE

Inese Viktorija Grospine, project coordinator at the Ministry of Environmental Protection and Regional Development of the Republic of Latvia, testifies that co-creation was first introduced in the organisation through an experiment with the state portal. Citizens were invited to participate in brainstorm sessions with paper prototypes, with the objective to bring in multiple perspectives on the type of information which should be provided on the portal. Inese testifies that a lot of requirements were collected and that citizens were at first confused with its new design. At the end of the process, they learnt that it is important to keep ownership of the process, and that different teams should work very closely together in order to implement the identified requirements:

'A successful co-creation process is when you have a notion of all needs and limitations of all stakeholders. It takes a lot of time, much more than traditional approaches. You need to come quickly to a joint decision and be careful that too many different opinions do not slow down the process'.

The general idea of involving citizens in service innovation fits into the philosophy of the public administration. They are an open ministry and the engagement with stakeholders helps them to think outside the box. However, it challenged their ways of working – as there are certain sets of rules to be followed. In this sense, caution should be raised about the difference between co-creation capabilities and its vision: 'Execution and practical application of skills is where it can be more challenging than the outlining of the philosophy'.

Inese Viktorija Grospine, project coordinator at the
Ministry of Environmental Protection and Regional
Development of the Republic of Latvia

NOTE

1. https://www.portodigital.pt/en/homepage/

Chapter 6

ORGANISATIONS IN TRANSITION

In recent years, attention has increasingly been turned to 'organisational culture' as a means to better understand and measure the success, or failings of public service and its delivery (Genc, 2017; Hofstede, 2001; Schein, 2004). This is grounded in the idea that effective strategy implementation leads to improved organisational performance since research has shown that implementation style is essential in steering strategies towards good organisational results (Goh & Arenas, 2020; Höglund & Mårtensson, 2019; Tuurnas, Stenvall, Virtanen, Pekkola, & Kurkela, 2019). Yet, public-sector organisations (PSOs) are said to often struggle with the implementation of strategies in practice, or, arguably, with the generation and capturing of value at the pace of the industry, particularly as more stakeholders become involved in these offerings, the governance of such complex, so-called value networks, becomes increasingly challenging (Borghys et al., 2020). This book's premise is that the application of public value co-creation in the context of the city – supported by business model, value network, and ecosystem thinking – facilitates the development of strategies for local governments that are sticky, promote public interest, and are, possibly better adapted to market conditions (cf. von Hippel, 2005).

In putting forward co-creation ideals, attention is drawn to dynamic organisational boundaries, indicative of a particular choice for an organisational culture corresponding to certain sets of behaviours and beliefs. More specifically, organisational culture is about the climate, practices and adopted values, such as underlying assumptions, expectations, taken for granted values, and collective memories, organisations develop around their employees (Cameron & Quinn, 2011). While an organisation's culture is seen as complex and difficult to distil, it is commonly accepted that it is a crucial factor in accomplishing strategic goals and positive performance in organisations, thereby providing a sense of identity to employees and unspoken direction for how to get on in the organisation (O'Riordan, 2015). In particular, the notion of values, such as impartiality, loyalty, equity, accountability and fairness, is pertinent within the public service realm (Vandenabeele, 2007). In recent years, however, value conflicts have materialised in the modernisation of public services, especially those associated with so-called New Public Management (NPM) reforms that aimed at obtaining greater efficiency and effectiveness within the public services domain (MacCarthaigh, 2008). Different operating environments between private-sector mantras and public service organisations that are also faced with constraints imposed by the various objectives of government or political authority, make it harder to establish a cultural change to facilitate a shift in public service values.

With this, coinciding with a 'smart city' trajectory, public service organisations find themselves tasked or challenged to capture creative and collaborative innovation across their organisational boundaries. In other words, through (direct) interactions between public bodies, private actors and other stakeholders, such as citizens, they must identify and tackle new relational complexities between actors, complex societal challenges in a local context and ever-growing data streams (e.g., linked open data, internet of things). In this view, PSOs have become part of a multi-stakeholder ecosystem of vertical and horizontal cooperation highlighting the interdependence and interaction of collaboration, collectivity and contextuality (Walravens, 2016). In short, the multi-stakeholder ecosystem is a network which arises from simultaneous attempts by diverse actors to co-create value bilaterally or as a group (Gyrd-Jones & Kornum, 2013). Emerging from the private sector, this concept is increasingly used in the public sector to describe the necessary cultural shift which organisations need in order to improve its institutions and performance. For example, by influencing employee behaviour and providing better customer service, public value co-creation spurs a consideration of the expansion of and operation across organisational boundaries facilitating organisational learning from citizens and other stakeholders (cf. Carlile, 2004; Oborn & Dawson, 2010). The relationship between organisational culture and performance in (both the private and) the public sector has received systematic attention, especially in terms of the direct effects of culture on performance (Arnaboldi & Azzone, 2010; Arundel, Bloch, & Ferguson, 2019; Nitzl, Sicilia, & Steccolini, 2019). To date, however, there are less empirical insights available about how to effectively transition to a multi-stakeholder ecosystem with dynamic boundaries wherein PSOs are increasingly operating so as to develop better, more efficient and longer-lasting public services in the urban setting (cf. Chapter 5).

This chapter seeks to shed light on the organisational culture in PSOs, particularly by drawing out the mechanisms of organisational culture, and the aspects of change involving a co-creation trajectory, thereby elaborating a multi-stakeholder perspective across organisational boundaries. In doing so, it can help PSOs tackle questions not only about their intra-organisational focus but also about their inter-organisational relationships. For this purpose, the *Co-creation Readiness Compass* is proposed and can be used as guidance in strategising public value co-creation, shaping of the authorising environment and operational capacity building.

6.1. STRATEGIC MANAGEMENT AND ORGANISATIONAL CULTURE IN THE PUBLIC SECTOR

For over two decades, a kind of 'administrative culture' seems to persist that characterises public organisation management by the processes of change (or, transition). Various terms have been used to describe the change trajectory, including managerialism (Pollit, 1990), entrepreneurial government (Osborne & Gaebler, 1992), market-based public administration (Lan & Rosenbloom, 1992), post-bureaucratic paradigm (Barzelay, 1992), and new public management (Hood, 1991). The latter term has been widely used to address the ever-growing public sector and complexities it has been confronted with by introducing 'economics' (such as transaction costs and public choice theory) and 'business management mechanisms' to the public-sector domain (Graham et al., 2019). The idea was that such a perspective would enhance the viability of long-term goals and effectiveness of public organisations while also taking measurements and performance standards into account (Pollitt & Bouckaert, 2017). In this view, strategic management – a mechanism in the private and public sphere to enhance the overall strategy process and organisational performance and, as such, organisational effectiveness – for public and private organisations may seem to have become less distinctive. Yet, the former tends to work towards preserving or reinforcing the fit between the organisation and its external stakeholders, strategically planning for outcomes associated with a specific setting of mandates, values and vision, while private organisations are very much orientated towards profitability and competition within a particular market (Andrews, Beynon, & Genc, 2017).

More recently, NPM seems to be superseded by what has been termed 'new public governance' (NPG) models (Dunleavy, Margetts, Bastow, & Tinkler, 2006).

The transition towards NPG is characterised not only by efficiency and effectiveness in government agencies that prioritise the participation of key stakeholders in policymaking but also by horizontal relationships between governmental agencies and private and non-profit organisations. In this development, strategic management – in all its variations – has become a common tool for public managers to create value and shape organisations (Ferlie & Ongaro, 2015). Thus, public strategic management operates in a multistakeholder environment of political and market dynamics underpinned by internal organisational and external stakeholders' capabilities that resource and operationalise public power to achieve benefits for individual groups of citizens and society as a whole. It is, therefore, important to set compatible strategic targets 'across boundaries' so as to enhance the application of resources in relation to objectives (Rainey, 2014; cf. 'mission economy' in Mazzucato (2021) and 'open innovation' in Chesbrough et al. (2006). Yet, insufficient attention has been given in the public-sector strategic management literature to such an holistic approach (George, Desmidt, Cools, & Prinzie, 2018). Available conceptual frameworks tend to point to the variances of several key components, such as content, process, context, outcome, operation, system and action (Bryson & Bromiley, 1993).

In considering the relationship between strategic management and the performance of PSOs, the content, processes and performance model, has proved useful. It highlights the phases of formulation and (rational and incremental) implementation vis-à-vis organisational performance (Andrews, Boyne, Law, & Walker, 2011). The formulation, or content making of strategy concerns 'the patterns of service provision that are selected and implemented by organizations' to achieve desired goals (Walker & Andrews, 2015, p. 231). Moreover, it is associated with the beliefs and values of an organisation and its employees. Nowadays, this strategy-making process is no longer considered to be a linear process (Pettigrew, Thomas, & Whittington, 2002).

Many models of strategy implementation can be detected in the literature, particularly, the rational and incremental approaches have gained traction. The rational approach is prescriptive and steers 'what an organization is, what it does, and why it does it' (Bryson, 1995, p. 20) by connecting strategic analysis, strategic development and strategy implementation. The incremental approach can be distinguished by trial, learning, experimentation and discussion, which is said to more naturally shape a set of behaviours over time, creating commitment while allowing flexibility among managers (Mintzberg, Ahlstrand, & Lampel, 1998) – associated with the so-called 'science of muddling through' (Lindblom, 1959). Strategy implementation, an essential yet difficult phase in the strategy process, concerns 'putting strategies into practice', such as planning and delivering services, organisational structures, evaluation systems, and is thus used to ensure capacities and performance standards (Ferlie & Ongaro, 2015). A successful strategy implementation is, arguably, equivalent to the chosen implementation style, which in turn is equivalent to organisational performance (Hupe & Hill, 2016).

In this, organisational culture has been found to be an important driver of organisational performance, drawing on the premise that a particular type of culture corresponds to enhancing certain objectives and goals (Wynen & Verhoest, 2015). The application of the term organisational culture spans several decades, and the traces of the idea go back even further, yet, to date, there is no commonly accepted definition (Deal & Kennedy, 1982; Jaques, 1951). From understanding organisational culture as an objective entity to a variable and metaphor, in particular, Schein's seminal levels model has often been used to understand better the various components of organisational culture (Schein, 2004; cf. Schneider & Barbera, 2014). The model distinguishes between artefacts, espoused beliefs and values, and underlying basic assumptions, affording the disentangling of culture's complexities.[1] Other widely used models include seven characteristics of organisational culture (Robbins, 2005) and the Competing Values Framework (CVF) (Cameron & Quinn, 2011). What these models seem to have in common with other streams of thought that seek to capture 'culture', is that they broadly seem to follow the approach of 'something shared by all members' such as common values and practices. The integration of the various dimensions of organisational culture can be summed up by:

> The organizational/corporate culture construct: it is (1) holistic, (2) historically determined, (3) related to anthropological concepts, (4) socially constructed, (5) soft, and (6) difficult to change. (Hofstede, Neuijen, Ohayv, & Sanders, 1990, p. 286)

In this view, culture can represent a sense of identity of the organisation's members. Also, the culture of an organisation is shaped by a long-term historical heritage, a so-called 'invisible hand' in public management, which also may mean that culture may be difficult to change (Rong & Hongwei, 2012). Furthermore, culture is associated with social and anthropological domains and can be explained by 'organizations have cultures' or 'organizations are cultures' (Cameron & Quinn, 2011). Moving from the components to types of culture, attention has been given to understanding cultures as strong or weak. Perhaps unsurprisingly, a strong organisational culture tends to result in a stronger business performance under stable conditions, yet this may be downplayed by the effects of 'groupthink' and change-orientation capacity under changing conditions (Sorensen, 2002). Notwithstanding these different streams of thought, organisational culture remains frequently debated in terms of how difficult it is to change because group members tend to appreciate stability (Nica, 2013). As, here, the relationship between the operational side of culture and the performance of the organisations are the focal point, a functionalist approach to examine organisational culture is useful (Hatch & Cunliffe, 2006; cf. symbolic and postmodernist perspectives in Genc, 2017).

While various models can be detected to investigate the relationships between organisational culture and performance, the CVF is one of the most widely used and empirically validated models (Gambi, Boer, Gerolamo, Jørgensen, & Carpinetti, 2015; for other models in the public sector see, e.g., Claver-Cortés, Llopis, Gascó, Manchón, & Flor, 1999). It has a track record in multi-method, cross-cultural research in exploring the culture of public-sector organisations. Since the development of three value dimensions (organisational focus, organisational structure, and organisational means-ends), the CVF has been employed to investigate what makes organisations effective, yielding insights into how to facilitate change in organisational culture, thereby enabling the integration of most organisational culture dimensions (Cameron & Quinn, 2011; Quinn & Rohrbaugh, 1983). The CVF consists of a set of organisational effectiveness indicators along two axes. These are control versus flexibility, and internal versus external focus. Organisations with an internal orientation tend to stress integration and communication, and, in contrast, those with an external orientation tend to emphasise growth, acquisition and interaction across organisational boundaries. From this, four major types, or models of culture have been derived, namely clan, adhocracy, market, and hierarchy culture (Cameron & Quinn, 2011). Clan culture has an internal, flexible and collaborative orientation emphasising value and goal sharing, cohesion, participation, individuality, and a sense of 'we-ness', associated with consensus, accountability, transparency (the explicit criteria of reward allocation), and equity (fairness of reward allocation). Adhocracy culture has an external, flexible and 'create' focus pointing to a dynamic, temporary, specialised setting associated with an innovation stimulus supported by adaptability, flexibility, and creativity in an uncertain climate. Market culture has an external, controlled and 'compete' orientation steered at transactions with external constituencies such as suppliers, customers and regulators. Hierarchy culture has an internal, controlled and control focus, underpinning a clear organisational structure, standardised rules and procedures, strict control, and distinct responsibilities associated with efficiency, effectiveness, accountability and rule of law (Yu & Wu, 2009).

The framework is supported by the Organisational Culture Assessment Instrument (OCAI),[2] which assists in evaluating dominant characteristics, organisational leadership, management of employees, organisation glue, strategic emphases and success criteria. In doing so, it reveals common approaches to work, shared assumptions and core values reflected in the four culture types (Heritage, Pollock, & Roberts, 2014). Thus, each continuum comprises a core value that is opposite from the value at the other end of the continuum, resulting in both distinctive and contradictory culture quadrants helping managers to navigate and reflect on their organisation culture. Often, these reveal that different models exist simultaneously, and which are indicative of showing if a culture is in line with strategic objectives (or, preferred situation), or mark the direction in which to change (Parker & Bradley, 2000). Particularly, as relationships between performance and culture have taken a main position in the public-sector context following a trajectory of reform initiatives, the CVF helps to yield insights into the relationship between specific types of culture and their related performance outcomes; for example, market-oriented culture in public-sector organisations is said to generate citizen satisfaction, while adhocracy-oriented culture is steered towards public service innovation (Walker, Avellaneda, & Berry, 2011).

Amidst determinants like personnel, motivation and team factors, the dynamics between leadership style and shaping organisation culture are thus particularly understood as significant determinants influencing the performance of PSOs in public service delivery (Moynihan & Pandey, 2010; see also 'good governance' in, e.g., Grindle, 2010). As outlined earlier, PSOs are multi-faceted collections of various entities with clear-cut mandates and different scales of operation and their reforms are strongly linked to beliefs, values, and practices underpinning conceptualisations that embody effectiveness criteria, outcomes and results. The literature has shown, however, that PSOs often seem to 'fail to learn', that is, to actually put the performance information gathered to good use beyond mere reporting objectives, or understanding and handling it well in the operation of various cultures existing in parallel throughout the organisation and, increasingly, across (and intra-)organisational boundaries (O'Riordan, 2015). This multi-stakeholder context associated with a shift from NPM to NPG (Osborne, 2006) implies a change in the way public administrations, implicitly and explicitly, navigate how to best contribute to the common good, sparking a prominent interest in the concept of public value as 'there is no more important topic in public administration and policy than public values' (Jørgensen & Bozeman, 2007, p. 355). Value in the public services realm is perhaps becoming a 'buzzword' (Cluley, Parker, &

Radnor, 2020) and this warrants a closer look at the recent, so-called public value turn.

6.2. THE PUBLIC VALUE TURN

What constitutes value and public value and how it emerges are informed by various disciplines which approach the public value question from a variety of perspectives, such as philosophy, economics, innovation and administrative studies (Mazzucato & Ryan-Collins, 2019; Ostrom, 1972; Prahalad & Ramaswamy, 2000; Vargo & Lusch, 2008). The meaning of the value concept is contested, such as who and what create values, generally, however, value tends to be seen as subjective, contextual and temporal, and while as a public service delivery directed at 'the common good' its impact can be considered both positively and negatively by the stakeholders involved (Cluley & Radnor, 2020). One seminal stream of thought in this regard was framed as the public value approach in public management. This work can be seen as a response to NPM that is associated with a rather managerial approach to the public sector. As a reaction to some of the deep reductions in government spending, Moore (1995) called for a better definition of public value as a key differentiator, but also legitimisation, for a sector that is said to generate value not being met by private actors. More specifically, the public value management literature has shown public value is often conceptualised differently to notions of value in the private sector and, hence, requires different theories and processes of actualisation of value (Stoker, 2006).

In contrast to the private sphere where managers create private value by generating profits through production and sales, what the public-sector manager must do to generate public value is less clear (Moore, 1995). The public sector must simultaneously meet the demands of diverse stakeholders and as such, what constitutes public value is obfuscated, and therefore more difficult to measure. Despite these differences, generating both public and private value involves costs. Importantly, while the value that they gain from a commercial service is usually clear to the consumer, the public sector can draw on the obligatory system of taxation to secure the resources required to create public value. Herein lies the challenge for public managers: in a society that emphasises private consumption, individual liberty, and private entrepreneurship as the main driver of development and progress, not only are public managers tasked with generating public value, they must also prove that their results are worth the citizen's sacrifice of private consumption and individual choice (Moore, 1995).

In the representative forms of government, it is assumed that all members of society can collectively set governmental priorities, and what resources are required. As a result, the responsibility for defining collective purposes, which will in turn influence what is understood as public value, is put with politics. Public managers must provide goods and services that citizens value which are not being met through market mechanisms. At the same time, they must maintain a 'proper distribution of rights and responsibilities between public and private organisations' (Moore, 1995, p. 52). In other words, public value is a result of a range of conceptualisations of value as utility or worth (Alford, Douglas, Geuijen, & 't Hart, 2017). This emphasises the critical role that governments at all play levels in mediating between citizens, companies and other actors, and that their actions produce value in the form of positive externalities. Moore's 'strategic triangle' underpins where public value emerges at the intersection of three mutually dependent processes: (1) defining public value (strategic goal definition); (2) creating the 'authorising environment' (coalition formation of multi stakeholders from the public, private and third sectors who support the strategic goal); and, (3) creating operational capacity (guaranteeing capacity at the operational level so as to execute the goal). More specifically, it was meant to describe what public managers should do, making the model less suited for representing more complex processes of public innovation that involve multiple stakeholders (Benington & Moore, 2011; Bryson, Sancino, Benington, & Sørensen, 2017; Hansen & Fuglsang, 2020; see also public value account in Moore, 2013 and public value process mapping in Alford & Yates, 2014). Elaborating on Moore's point, Bozeman (2002) speaks of public values and which concerns shared ideas about citizen's rights and benefits, their duties to society and the state, and the basis of government decision-making and policy provision (Bozeman, 2007).

While there certainly is a lot of debate about the ways in which these concepts can be interpreted, taken together, public value can be understood as something that can be measured and experienced, while public values are indicative of a kind of ethos (Cluley & Radnor, 2020). Furthermore, within these public value conceptualisations, public managers are often positioned at the forefront of the (complex) value trajectory (Bryson et al., 2017; Moore, 1995). For example, public goods like the open data that (local) governments make available to citizens and the market can generate additional value when put into use as a new app and or a service created by a small medium enterprise (Walravens, 2016). There are a range of value-generating activities with clear economic and social potentialities, which can be built on the back of this public good. Moving more into the 'across boundaries' thinking is Benington's conceptualisation of the new role of government associated with 'networked community governance':

> One of the biggest challenges facing governments in a networked, multilevel, polycentric society is how to 'lead' not only in partnership with other levels of government and with organisations from other sectors, but also with active involvement from informal associations, community groups and individual citizens. The role of government in this kind of situation is increasingly being seen not simply as to act as referee between competing interest groups, but also to work proactively to try to develop some kind of shared vision or common purpose out of the diversity of perspectives, and to negotiate and mobilise coalitions of interest to achieve communal aims. (Benington, 2011, pp. 36–37)

In this view, the meaning of public value gets double articulated in its relation to the public sphere as it leads to a wider understanding of public value, encompassing both what is the public value and what adds value to the public sphere (Benington, 2011; Benington & Moore, 2011). In this sense, public value is 'direct', as it serves the public's immediate interests and manifests through citizen engagement in governing. When citizens are empowered to more actively engage with government, the values that they co-create can act also as a countervailing force to those values generated through conventional top-down processes that tend to dominate governance, even urban governance, which is the level of government that operates closest to the people. Through a complex deliberative process (Dryzek, 2002), existing imbalances in power relations are re-negotiated, new ideas are introduced into governance, and public voice becomes integrated into long-term government planning, an 'indirect' type of public value which is co-created through the direct expression of public intent and interest. Public value can be seen in terms of what is currently valued by citizens and communities and of what will be the public interest from a longer-term perspective (Benington, 2015). The public sphere, therefore, results from certain democratic practices. This draws attention to the seemingly dichotomous roles of political and public managers who are willing to take up additional tasks (beyond the original description) so as to achieve a net value benefit for citizens in learning what they actually want (Alford et al., 2017). In doing so, a shift away from an intra-organisational orientation to a more dispersed leadership model of multi-stakeholder or actor collaboration becomes apparent, where procedural rationality is less sought after than innovation and public value creation (OECD, 2019).

Thus, public value theory evolved from Moore's focus on the value added by PSOs and public managers, to a wider understanding of political, economic and social processes. Particularly, highlighting societal values associated with judgements about creating public value, a psychological approach on the human activity of valuing (Meynhardt, 2009), and public value as part of the public sphere, specially, in terms of contested democratic processes (Hartley, Parker, & Beashel, 2019). Yet, more research is needed to better understand as well as systematically and empirically investigate the more complex, collective and democratic processes of public value creation (see e.g., Living Labs in Hansen & Fuglsang, 2020) that involve multiple stakeholders (Alford & Yates, 2014; Bryson et al., 2017). In this line, co-creation in the urban context highlights public value creation foremost (but not only) as 'a societal value created through contested democratic processes between relevant stakeholders seeking to deal with "wicked" public problems' (Hansen & Fuglsang, 2020, p. 3; cf. Bryson et al., 2017; Hartley et al., 2019). Public value creation is thus 'operationalised' by public-sector actors in a multi-actor context – moving thus from a mainly intra-organisational focus to one on inter-organisational relationships – whereby markets are co-shaped in line with public purpose facilitating public, private and civil society sectors to collaborate in tackling and solving societal problems (Mazzucato & Ryan-Collins, 2019). The next section draws specific attention to public value co-creation in a multi-stakeholder setting, which is followed by the Co-creation Readiness Compass that can be used to strategise public value definition, creation of the authorising environment and operational capacity building.

6.3. PUBLIC VALUE CO-CREATION AS ASSEMBLAGE

In the value co-creation literature (cf. Chapter 2), attention is increasingly shifting from examining the role of 'encounters' and 'experiences' between providers and consumers to complex and multi-actor systems (Payne et al., 2008; Prahalad & Ramaswamy, 2004). While such value creation paradigms were previously seen as (more) linear in today's intertwined setting of stakeholders, 'value network thinking' has been put forward to understand a multi-stakeholder setting as 'relatively self-contained, self-adjusting system of resource-integrating actors connected by shared institutional arrangements and mutual value creation through service exchange' (Vargo & Lusch, 2016, p. 161; cf. Porter, 1980). The outcome map of the value network analysis shows how interactions occur between stakeholders throughout the entire ecosystem and what meaningful service streams can be identified. While, to date, not much insights are available about value co-creation in terms of actors' engagement, factors and outcomes in value co-creation in complex service systems, the roles of public, private, voluntary, and informal community sectors, including citizens, have to also be taken into account in defining and advancing public value both separately and jointly under strategic perspective (Bryson et al., 2017).

In order to move the discussion and practice forward about public value and its multi-stakeholder co-creation process in PSOs, the ontological underpinnings offered by 'assemblage' are useful (Cluley & Radnor, 2020). Taken at face value, co-production and co-creation are attractive ideas in governance, which is why these practices are implicitly considered as 'best practice' in service provision. However, there is great variation in what activities and ideas fall under the umbrella concept of public value as it is actualised through either of these distinct processes. The tendency to use co-production and co-creation interchangeably engenders confusion about co-creation which can, to some degree, explain its misuse and underuse in urban governance today (Voorberg et al., 2015). While co-production emphasises the value creation potential of the public sector, and how it is embedded in the relationship between public service and the end-user that is necessitated by public service delivery, it still rests on linear, top-down processes of service production (Radnor, Osborne, Kinder, & Mutton, 2014). In contrast, co-creation is 'an interactive and dynamic relationship whereby value is created at the nexus of interaction' (Osborne, 2018, p. 225). These interactions generate value for both service users and government via a non-linear production process that is informed by service users' 'wider experience of life' (Osborne, 2018). A first step towards moving from theory to realisation through practice, or praxis, in terms of co-creation is to interrogate the epistemology and ontology underlying the co-creation/co-production concept.

As a starting point, it is useful to examine current discussions on co-creation that emphasise how parties engaged in a multi-stakeholder environment experience value. Less emphasis is placed on the particular nature and mandate of public administration, which critically shapes the environment under which co-creation takes place, that is in the domain embodied by public administration. Public administration has the responsibility of simultaneously meeting a vast array of public needs from education to urban planning, and since a profit motive is usually absent (these goods and services are not excludable and/or exhaustible) the services that they provide rarely are sufficiently met by the private sphere (Cluley & Radnor, 2020). What is more, public administration often provides moral leadership and initiates the diffusion of norms related to goods, which represent a trade-off between profit in the short run and wellbeing in the long run, like healthcare and sustainability. Finally, the public sphere provides a level of stability that is essential to the fiduciary system underlying business exchange, therefore, the private sector is both a direct and indirect beneficiary of the co-creation of public value. Given the ubiquity of these services, it is clear that the public sector represents the entire public, despite the heterogeneity therein (Deleuze & Guattari, 1987). And yet despite its uniqueness and the logics inherent to the public sphere (March & Olsen, 2011), managerial techniques and strategies conventional in the private sphere are increasingly transplanted into the public administration, a trend that is encapsulated in NPM. Indeed, the emergence of value co-production has been framed as a reprisal against NPM, which emphasises the importance of value experiences of the public sectors and the constituents it serves, which lie beyond concerns of mere efficiency and efficacy (Osborne, Radnor, Kinder, & Vidal, 2015).

While both co-production and co-creation find their origins in service-dominant logic (SDL), their evolution from this shared root has largely been philosophy agnostic. In the case of value co-creation, the absence of an explicit philosophical foundation has been noted. In response, Cluley and Radnor (2020) have leveraged a Deleuzo and Guattari (1987) perspective, which brings to bear the idea of assemblage to public value co-creation. In an assemblage, public value co-creation abandons the logic of the unitary entity (Nail, 2017) like, for example, 'the public', to consider the multiple voices that make up the constellation of actors whose linkages with one another give rise to the multi-stakeholder ecosystem. Importantly, the structure of this assemblage is fluid (Deleuze & Guattari, 1987). That is, it continuously evolves as different actors resting within positions in the network are activated or become dormant. This conceptualisation of co-creation distinguishes itself from co-production by shifting the emphasis from outcome to process. It achieves this by emphasising the relationship between (service) user and service provider, which is both reciprocal (Grönroos, 2011) and dynamic (Osborne, 2018) and rests on the value generation potential of both public administration and the public service user, rather than that of public administration. In other words, it emphasises multiplicity, which in turn emphasises the constant renegotiation of relationships between public administration and the different publics they serve. Given its dynamism, value co-creation can simultaneously generate value for different people according to their needs.

The changeability of value, which relies both on the changing needs of service users as well as the changing nature of relationships that they share with public administration, as well as with each other, as mutual beneficiaries of value. Value, then, can be gauged based on how the interaction with the government shapes the wider (lived) experience of the service user as well as of the service provider, which in this case is government. This emerging view on value co-creation ushers in new questions related to the administration of public services as well as its advancement over time, such as about the essence and dimensions of value in this realm, individual-collective equilibrium, and processes for determining value among multiple stakeholders and agendas. In particular it must be noted that not much attention has been given thus far to the extent to which value creation is accessible and meaningful, or, in other words, not everyone is (or wants to be) included nor benefits from public service value generated (Cluley et al., 2020). In following the logic of assemblage, public value is understood in terms of a dynamic relationship in which – in a continuum of – 'positive' and 'negative' exist side-by-side (see 'disvalue' in Esposito & Ricci, 2015). More specifically, co-creation ideals tend to be (perhaps, intuitively so) associated with enhanced public service design and delivery, thus, users participating in co-creation activities result in better services (Osborne, 2018). Yet, such 'ethos' is indicative of a 'theory-practice' division due to the complexity and materiality of the organisation of public services (Cluley & Radnor, 2020). Furthermore, insights have emerged showing that drivers such as socio-economic status and environmental factors tend to be ignored, consequently, 'the inclusivity of public value creation processes are often exclusive in practice' (Cluley et al., 2020, p. 2). By intersecting public value co-creation with assemblage, the continuum of value creation and experiences can be considered, challenged and possibly remedied.

6.4. CO-CREATION READINESS COMPASS

As outlined in this chapter, a multi-stakeholder approach to public value co-creation has evolved from new ways of thinking about government activity, policymaking, and service delivery associated with a shift from effectiveness and efficiency ('results') management to the management of value as a collective effort ('relationships') (Benington & Moore, 2011; Bryson et al., 2017; Moore, 1995). In this way, it clearly addresses a need to investigate more complex interactions between various actors, domains, and practices as a basis for public value creation, while seeking to reinforce democracy (Bryson et al., 2017). Also, this avenue has yielded new ways of thinking about innovation in the public sector, understanding it as a practice and platform for generating and negotiating public value devoted to democratic principles (see 'responsible innovation' in Stilgoe et al., 2013). Innovation is thus understood as a collaborative and distributed process wherein multiple stakeholders investigate and develop solutions to shared challenges 'across boundaries' highlighting inter-organisational relationships (Sørensen &

Torfing, 2017; van der Graaf, 2018b). This has given rise to new ways of conducting and managing co-creation between citizens, public administration, civil society, and the private sector. Supported by claims like 'participatory governance initiatives' and 'citizen engagement' such innovation practices – associated with 'networked governance' – have not only been used to promote public-sector development but also tied to advance the perceptions of democracy (cf. Chapter 2). Furthermore, public value co-creation has been put forward as a fluid process which elaborates a more inclusive and a value-continuum perspective.

There is no doubt about the relevance to furthering conceptualisations, yet, how best to measure value and co-creation is less obvious. For example, in the private sector various instruments can be detected including sustainability indicators, corporate responsibility rankings, and shared value measures and whether these are the right ones, is unclear. More specifically, some, like the Public Value Scorecard (PVSC) emphasise value creation in financial, moral, political and aesthetic value (Meynhardt, 2015). It may be used as a tool for monitoring and evaluating performance or for engaging in dialogue with stakeholders who can use the PVSC to understand what, if any, social values are generated by a company's activities, delivered in a decent manner, its political acceptability, and how consumers experience it. Another, the Public Value Toolkit (PVT) (Bloomberg Harvard; city leadership initiative, 2020) moves from the individual to the group, and emphasises inclusiveness in its three, related foci: the outcomes that are jointly pursued (public value), the pathways or means towards achieving these outcomes (operational capacity) and the various sources or support that can be mobilised to encourage people to take these pathways (legitimacy and support). In short, the PVT couples means with ends in value-co-creation.

While the PVSC focusses on human needs and the PVT on means, ends and strategies, the Leipzig Leadership Model examines public value from the standpoint of public value leadership (Kirchgeorg, Meynhardt, Pinkwart, Suchanek, & Zülch, 2017). Leadership is an important contributor to public-sector innovation, especially in local government (Hambleton & Howard, 2013). Since public value, as emphasised by the PVT, essentially emerges from a complex creative and collective process. Collective processes require steering, guidance, and management. In other words, it requires leadership. Leadership is particularly fundamental during moments of crisis and system change, when groups and communities need a shared purpose or vision. A shared purpose encourages individuals to set aside personal interest and short-term thinking and to invest in public value creation.

Another focus can be detected on 'multi-stakeholderism' as such, or multi-stakeholder (or 'hybrid') orchestration approach to address interdependencies between different issue spaces and scales of action (spatial, temporal, etc.) to overcome complexities in today's society (Reypens, Lievens, & Blazevic, 2021). As a consequence of these interdependencies, many different actors are affected by public value co-creation, and, therefore, must be included in the process. The intersection of these actors' interests (e.g., they may jointly benefit from public value or the benefit of one actor may come at a cost to another) gives rise to a network of interactions (Freeman, 1984) which can be represented and analytically unpacked as a multi-stakeholder network (Roloff, 2008). Multi-stakeholder (or 'hybrid') orchestration, therefore, refers to a new type of management, which must be sufficiently agile to react to the inherent dynamism of networks, which can easily transform as new stakeholders join and others leave (cf. Business Model Matrix in Ballon, 2007; principles of Transition in Geels & Schot, 2010).

In sum, a wide range of instruments have been developed to measure and support value co-creation. The existence of many, diverse tools enable a multi-actor approach to public value co-creation in/by the public sector. In this multi-actor approach, an inter- and intra-organisational 'culture' must be established and supported by managers and a broad base of stakeholders including employees working in different departments. It must also involve trans-boundary collaboration. The *Co-creation Readiness Compass* pictured in Fig. 4 can be used – in addition to the methods and tools presented, particularly, in Chapter 4 – as a guidance tool to kick-start the organisation's readiness to establish and integrate co-creation as a capacity within the public service organisation.

1.   *Towards a co-creation culture and attitude: define the organisational culture*

The first step in the Co-creation Readiness Compass is to reflect on the organisational culture in the public organisation. The organisational culture can be specifically defined by practices and adopted values, such as impartiality, loyalty, equity, etc., but it can also be implicit. An organisational culture provides a sense of identity to the employees, which gives them an unspoken direction for how to get on in the organisation.

Several frameworks were provided in this chapter to investigate the organisational culture in the public administration, such as the CVF (Cameron & Quinn, 2011) and the OCAI. In order to establish a supportive culture for co-creation in the organisation, it is important to investigate whether values such as flexibility, dynamics, and creativity are supported. These values are, for instance, represented in an 'adhocracy culture' (Cameron & Quinn, 2011).

This type of culture is steered towards public service innovation and shares core principles of co-creation (cf. Chapter 3).

The outcomes of the assessment can help in defining the 'readiness' of the current established organisation culture for organising co-creative processes for public service innovations. It is advised that the organisational culture supports (i) an open attitude towards collaboration with citizens, (ii) a willingness to listen to their ideas and (iii) to have an inclination to actively use the information for policymaking. The attitudes towards co-creation are acknowledged as essential for successful co-creation of the public services, both from the side of the professionals as the citizens (Brandsen et al., 2018). In this regard, Shamim, Ghazali, and Albinsson (2017) focus on three types of attitudes for measuring positive value creation between professionals and users. They measure the interaction attitude, or the willingness to respond positively to the influences in the process, and the knowledge sharing attitude, or the willingness to share knowledge during interaction to co-create value. The responsive attitude refers to the propensity to respond effectively to the requests of the organiser for engaging in dialogue to co-create value. Furthermore, besides attitudes, there should also be a willingness to listen and trust the collected information of citizens. Last, the organisational culture supports a commitment to adjust structures or procedures in order to take the citizen's input for granted.

In sum, the following leading questions can help in defining whether the organisational culture of PSOs, or a specific department, has a co-creation culture and attitude:

- What are the core values of the established organisational culture in the public administration, and is there a match with the core principles of co-creation?

- To what extent is there a high public service motivation for innovation and support for citizen participation?

- To what extent is there an open attitude towards collaboration with citizens, and what are the interaction, knowledge sharing and responsive attitudes?

- To what extent is there a willingness to listen to the ideas of citizens and an inclination to actively use the information?

- To what extent is there a trusted attitude in the citizens' input, and vis-à-vis: to what extent is there a feeling of reciprocity and trust by citizens in the public administration?

Last, it has to be noted that an organisational culture may be difficult to change, as it is shaped by long-standing habits and hierarchies. If the outcomes reveal that the organisation is not open towards or ready for establishing a co-creation culture, then a change trajectory in the longer term could be established that also identifies and tackles barriers for adoption (e.g., lack of clear proposition, methodology and innovation-orientated profiles, and low perception of priority, etc.).

2. *Have legitimacy and support: define the operational capacity and role play*

The second step in the Co-creation Readiness Compass is to gain legitimacy and support for co-creation in the public administration. To gain legitimacy, it is advised that a key responsible person, being a civil servant or an external expert, is appointed to support this operational change. The appointed person should have a holistic knowledge of the various dimensions of co-creation and delegate with other key actors in an established working group that spans multiple departments. Legitimacy should be gained both on the operational side, as well as on the policy side of the public administration. This can be done by showcasing good examples and by exemplifying projects that were identified in the working group as a possibility to enhance service innovation. These reports can be transferred to the aldermen, who, in turn, can also provide policy support for it. Furthermore, a good balance should be sought between old and new operational approaches of project implementation, whereby one could consider if co-creation should be implemented as a conditional requirement or not. Furthermore, in order to gain support for co-creation in the public administration, clear guidelines and protocols should be established in the working group. These guidelines and protocols reflect upon the following elements: (i) the operational capacity and role play of the public administration, (ii) the provision of material or personnel support and (iii) reinforcing capabilities in the public administration.

In terms of the operational capacity and role play of the public administration, different scenarios are possible. A public administration can decide to take up a more active or passive role in co-creation processes with citizens or other stakeholders. In this regard, Ansell and Torfing identified six different leadership roles for public value creation, being a sponsor, convener, facilitator, mediator, catalyst and implementer (2021, p. 216). As a sponsor, a public administration will secure support for the project in the network and promote the solutions, while as an implementer, a public administration will coordinate the actions and strive for service performance. Next, in terms of support, a public administration can decide to provide financial support to stakeholders for organising co-creative processes in the network of the public administration. It can also provide material support, such as the provision of meeting rooms for workshops, communication materials or sensor equipment. Last, it is important that the involved civil servants all have a clear definition on co-creation and are provided with guidelines on the usages of methods and tools (cf. Chapter 4). Sufficient time should be invested in training, in order to support any member to feel capable to contribute and set-up co-creation processes for a project. This also includes the understanding of the legal impacts of co-creation (e.g., General Data Protection Regulation [GDPR]).

In sum, the following leading questions can help in defining whether legitimacy and support are established in PSOs for supporting co-creation:

- To what extent is there legitimacy for implementing co-creation as a conditional requirement in an innovation project?

- What are exemplary projects in order to gain support for co-creation in public administration?

- What are the chosen leadership roles of public administration towards co-creation?

- To what extent is it possible to mobilise resources for setting up co-creation? Are there specific materials, financial resources or personnel support available?

- To what extent is there a shared understanding of terminology like co-creation, co-design, co-creation methods and tools, etc.? To what extent is there the ability to choose appropriate co-creation tools?

3. Towards co-creation readiness: define the action plan

The third step in the Co-creation Readiness Compass is the definition of an action plan. After gaining legitimacy and support for co-creation in the internal organisation, concrete action and experimentation should give insights into the opportunities and barriers of co-creation (cf. Chapter 5). It is advised that one starts at first with a short-term, ad-hoc co-creation activity and then evaluates the outcomes before scaling up towards a long-term sustained programme for public service innovation.

An action plan should help to explain the concrete steps of implementing co-creation and establishing citizen engagement in public service innovation.

A first concrete action is to adapt the public procurement procedures towards design principles (cf. Chapter 3). A standard procurement contract will define the requirements in advance, without the identification of users' needs – which is the opposite of service design processes. Therefore, PSOs need to reflect here whether they will hire external experts to apply methodologies, such as design thinking, or that they coordinate and implement the co-creation processes themselves. Secondly, guidelines and protocols need to be defined related to the set-up of the methodology. Citizens' input needs to be collected through interviews, personas, workshops, etc., and needs to be properly analysed and evaluated. The co-creation flowchart design (cf. Chapter 4) can help PSOs to determine the exact activities that need to be implemented, depending on the goal and maturity level of the innovation. Thirdly, a realistic and accurate assessment should be made of the problem for each specific project: what is the scope, its scale, the target group, the desired outcomes, etc. One should have a clear image of the processes, who benefits and who might be harmed from its implementation. Therefore, an understanding needs to be created on the individual level of each project, which could be summarised in a 'use case' description. Last, the action plan should also take notice of the learning capacities and abilities of the involved actors to integrate the insights coming from citizens and other external stakeholders. Therefore, for each project, one should decide on the leadership role of the public administration.

In sum, the following leading questions can help in defining the action plan for generating public value co-creation:

- To what extent can public procurement processes be adapted in order to involve external input?

- What is the desired methodology for the collection of feedback? Which activities and methods and tools can be implemented?

- To what extent is there a clear understanding of the desired public value?

- Is a 'use case' description defined for each project, which clearly describes the goals, the risks, target groups and the needed support and materials from the public administration?

- Is the chosen leadership role linked towards the desired public value?

4.   *Towards public value creation: consolidate and evaluate*

The final step in the co-creation readiness compass is to move towards public value creation with a consolidated strategy. This consolidated strategy should outline a clear vision on the creation of public value related to its changeability. As explained before, the creation of value is not fixed to a certain product or service but relies on the changing needs of users and the changing relationships of the PSO. This idea of 'assemblage' is fluid and should take the different stakeholders, agendas and time dimensions into account. Specific attention should also be given to the inclusive nature of the strategy: the outcomes that are jointly pursued, the means for achieving these outcomes and the various sources or support that are mobilised to encourage people to take part. Therefore, it is recommended to also communicate the consolidated strategy of the public administration with the public on the organisation's website, together with some exemplary projects and action plans. The published strategy sets the co-creation culture in stone and will help in the collaboration and management of expectations from the stakeholder network. Of course, in ideal circumstances this strategy comes before practice. If a PSO has no or limited experience with co-creation, then the lessons learned from phase 3 can help towards the consolidation of a strategy. Last, as context changes over time, it is also recommended to establish a monitoring, measuring, and evaluation process which periodically updates this strategy. The involvement of external stakeholders can also help in these assessment efforts.

In sum, the following leading questions can help in defining the consolidated strategy:

- To what extent is my strategy focussed on ad-hoc projects, or a consolidated long-term vision?

- To what extent does my strategy take into account the interchangeability of value creation?

- To what extent is the strategy inclusive towards different stakeholders in different contexts and times?

- What are potential key performance indicators for the monitoring, measuring and evaluation process?

- Are we available to provide a clear evidence base which demonstrates the opportunities of co-creation?

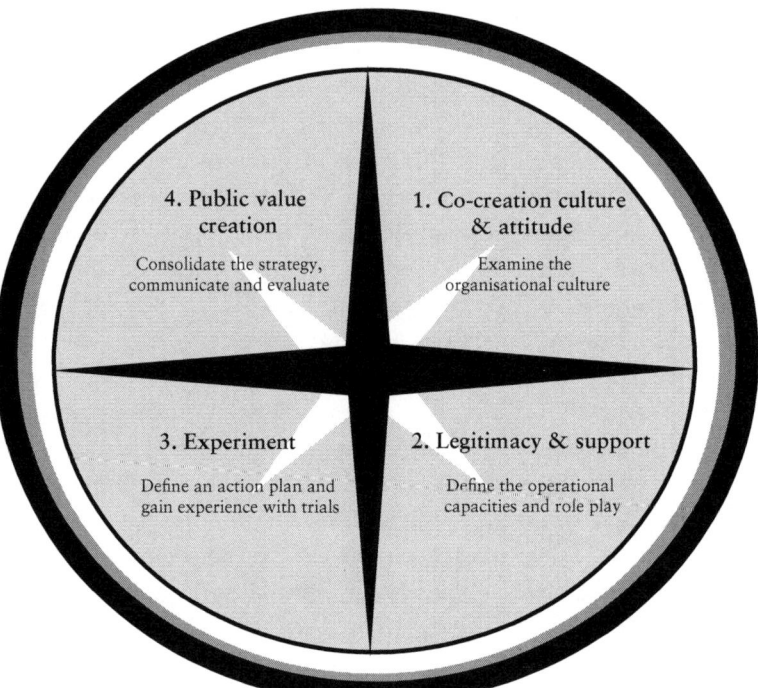

Fig. 3.   Co-creation Readiness Compass.

NOTES

1. The organisation's artefacts, such as logos, stories, and overt behaviours or members, are tangible items entailing the physical and social environment in which the organisation operates. Espoused beliefs and values are the more intangible elements like strategies, goals, ethical and moral codes and organisational ideology.

2. See, for example, https://www.ocai-online.com/ to conduct an OCAI for your organisation.

AFTERWORD

At heart, this book is about the promotion of co-creation as a way to plan, execute, and evaluate public service design and delivery for contemporary and future cities, supported by insights gained through years of experience with and research on co-creation as well as testimonials from practitioners. It has taken a close, and critical look at citizen participation in urban co-creation, unpacking the different ideas that undergird the concept to shed light on common barriers and risks associated with it. It then provides advice for avoiding these known pitfalls of public value co-creation first by presenting the '6C Framework', which identifies the core design principles for co-creation, and second by offering insights into useful tools and methods for co-creation. The testimonials demonstrate how such tools and principles can work in practice, and finally our 'Co-creation Readiness Compass' can be used as guidance in strategising public value co-creation, shaping of the authorising environment and operational capacity building.

Today's public-sector organisations have 'to do more with less', particularly at the local level where government services have the most direct impact on people's everyday lives. They are faced with 'wicked' problems and undergoing a paradigmatic shift associated with perpetuous technological developments – increasingly embedded into the systems and infrastructures that foster the built environment and governance dynamics – that are claimed to transform public service development and delivery. With these, public values are also recalibrating. Not only do city administrations work hard to keep up with these challenges but they also keep abreast with the changing expectations of citizens, and rapidly diversifying urban populations that make different claims on government. They explore ways to meet these new demands with a more robust value-based perspective on public service development and delivery. Co-creation is considered a valid means to support this 'balancing act' played out by cities and other public service organisations to boost efficient and cost-effective governance facilitated by endless 'smart' and 'collaborative innovation' solutions, while putting forward a citizen-centric focus that is sustainable over time. Manifested as smart cities, critical shifts in the discourse can be detected from promoting a technology focus, to a human and humane and, more recently, a rights-based perspective that aims at achieving a just city, and society more broadly (Breuer & Pierson, 2021). This demarcates the predominant conception of urban space as a market that mainly serves the interests of companies as well as states, captured by terms such as 'platform urbanism' (Barns, 2020; Graham et al., 2019; van der Graaf & Ballon, 2019) and is provoked by initiatives (including 'quadruple helix' thinking; Borghys et al., 2020) and bodies such as the European Innovation Partnership on Smart Cities and Communities (EIP-SCC).

The premise of this book is that structuring and formalising co-creation processes can bring together the various stakeholders to foster responsible innovation and a systemic, value-based approach to sustainable urban development. In this way, it supports the call to turn the attention away from smart cities as an embodiment of entrepreneurial urbanism in steering the transformation of the public sector away from tactical responses towards a systemic, value-based approach. Co-creation, in all its facets (such as assemblage, culture, dis/value), offers a point of departure to develop not only a multi-stakeholder perspective but also allows them to develop a relational one which can concern all kinds of relations, such as those of oppression (cf. Kitchin, 2021) as well as those of other species and non-living systems. A 'more-than-human' orientation can, for example, enable future co-creation trajectories with multispecies as well as machines, moving the exceptional and human-centred urban focus towards a more inclusive understanding and incorporation of designs for other 'others'. Working towards present and future cities that are more-than-human and just for all, the design of hybrid digital-physical urban spaces will need methods, tools, approaches, platforms, and so forth to engage different communities, environments, and all kinds of non-human entities and creatures. They will need a public-sector transformation, fuelled by radical changes in culture, mindset, and ideas about the citizen, the community, and the city.

REFERENCES

Acar, F., Raes, L., Rosseau, B., & Satta, M. (2021). Making policies with data: The legacy of the PoliVisu Project, pp. 105–122.

Agger, A. (2012). Towards tailor-made participation: How to involve different types of citizens in participatory governance. *The Town Planning Review*, *83*(1), 29–45.

Agusti, C., Bluestone, B., Carvalho, P., Cudden, J., Duvernet, C., Fitzgerald, J., … Williams, B. (2014). *Co-creating cities. Defining co-creation as a means of citizen engagement*. doi: 10.13140/RG.2.1.3684.5849

Alford, J., Douglas, S., Geuijen, K., & 't Hart, P. (2017). Ventures in public value management: Introduction to the symposium. *Public Management Review*, *19*(5), 589–604. doi: 10.1080/14719037.2016.1192160

Alford, J., & Yates, S. (2014). Mapping public value processes. *International Journal of Public Sector Management*, *27*(4), 334–352.

Almeida, V. A. F., Doneda, D., & da Costa, E. M. (2018). Humane smart cities: The need for governance. *IEEE Internet Computing*, *22*(2), 91–95. doi: 10.1109/MIC.2018.022021671

Almirall, E., Lee, M., & Wareham, J. (2012). Mapping living labs in the landscape of innovation methodologies. *Technology Innovation Management Review*, *2*, 12–18. doi: 10.22215/timreview/603

Alves, H. (2013). Co-creation and innovation in public services. *The Service Industries Journal*, *33*(7–8), 671–682. doi: 10.1080/02642069.2013.740468

Amabile, T. (2011). *Componential theory of creativity*. Boston, MA: Harvard Business School.

Andrews, R., Beynon, M., & Genc, E. (2017). Strategy implementation style and public service effectiveness, efficiency, and equity. *Administrative Sciences*, *7*(1), 4. MDPI AG. Retrieved from http://dx.doi.org/10.3390/admsci7010004

Andrews, R., Boyne, G. A., Law, J., & Walker, R. M. (2011). Strategy implementation and public service performance. *Administration & Society*, *43*(6), 643–671. doi: 10.1177/0095399711412730

Ansell, C., Doberstein, C., Henderson, H., Siddiki, S., & 't Hart, P. (2020). Understanding inclusion in collaborative governance: A mixed methods approach. *Policy and Society*, *39*(4), 570–591. doi: 10.1080/14494035. 2020.1785726

Ansell, C., & Gash, A. (2008). Collaborative governance in theory and practice. *Journal of Public Administration Research and Theory*, *18*(4), 543–571. doi: 10.1093/jopart/mum032

Ansell, C., & Torfing, J. (2021). *Public governance as co-creation: A strategy for revitalizing the public sector and rejuvenating democracy* (1st ed.). Cambridge: Cambridge University Press.

Arnaboldi, M., & Azzone, G. (2010). Constructing performance measurement in the public sector. *Critical Perspectives on Accounting*, *21*(4), 266–282. doi: 10.1016/j.cpa.2010.01.016

Arnstein, S. R. (1969). A ladder of citizen participation. *Journal of the American Institute of Planners*, *35*(4), 216–224. doi: 10.1080/ 01944366908977225

Arundel, A., Bloch, C., & Ferguson, B. (2019). Advancing innovation in the public sector: Aligning innovation measurement with policy goals. *Research Policy*, *48*(3), 789–798. doi: 10.1016/j.respol.2018.12.001

Auh, S., Bell, S. J., McLeod, C. S., & Shih, E. (2007). Co-production and customer loyalty in financial services. *Journal of Retailing*, *83*(3), 359–370.

Baccarne, B., Logghe, S., Schuurman, D., & De Marez, L. (2016). Governing quintuple helix innovation: Urban living labs and socio-ecological entrepreneurship. *Technology Innovation Management Review*, *6*(3), 22–30.

Baka, V. (2017). Co-creating an open platform at the local governance level: How openness is enacted in Zambia. *Government Information Quarterly*, *34*(1), 140–152. doi: 10.1016/j.giq.2016.10.001

Ballon, P. (2007). Business modelling revisited: The configuration of control and value. *Info*.

Baptista, N., Alves, H., & Matos, N. (2020). Public sector organizations and cocreation with citizens: A literature review on benefits, drivers, and barriers. *Journal of Nonprofit & Public Sector Marketing*, *32*(3), 217–241. doi: 10.1080/10495142.2019.1589623

Barns, S. (2020). *Platform urbanism: Negotiating platform ecosystems in connected cities*. Singapore: Palgrave Macmillan.

Barzelay, M. (1992). *Breaking through bureaucracy: A new vision for managing in government*. Berkeley, CA: University of California Press.

Bason, C. (2010). Leading public sector innovation: Co-creating for a better society.

Baumgartner, F. R., & Jones, B. D. (2010). *Agendas and instability in American Politics*. Chicago, IL: University of Chicago Press.

Benington, J. (2011). From private choice to public value. In J. Benington & M. H. Moore (Eds.), *Public value: Theory and practice* (pp. 31–51). New York, NY: Palgrave MacMillan.

Benington, J. (2015). Public value as a contested democratic practice. In J. Bryson, B. Crosby, & L. Bloomberg (Eds.), *Creating public value in practice* (pp. 29-48). Boca Raton, FL: Taylor & Francis.

Benington, J., & Moore, M. H. (2011). Public value in complex and changing times. In J. Benington & M. H. Moore (Eds.), *Public value: Theory and practice* (pp. 1–30). New York, NY: Palgrave MacMillan.

Benkler, Y. (2006). *The wealth of networks*. New Haven, CT: Yale University Press.

Bentzen, T. Ø. (2020). Continuous co-creation: How ongoing involvement impacts outcomes of co-creation. *Public Management Review*, 0(0), 1–21. doi: 10.1080/14719037.2020.1786150

BEPA. (2010). *Empowering people, driving change: Social innovation in the European Union*. Report prepared by A. Hubert, M. Bonifacio and J. Konings, Bureau of European Policy Advisers.

Blessing, L. T. M., & Chakrabarti, A. (2009). *DRM: A design research methodology*. London: Springer.

Bloch, C., & Bugge, M. M. (2013). Public sector innovation: From theory to measurement. *Structural Change and Economic Dynamics*, 27, 133–145. doi: 10.1016/j.strueco.2013.06.008

Bogers, M., Zobel, A.-K., Afuah, A., Almirall, E., Brunswicker, S., Dahlander, L., … Ter Wal, A. L. J. (2017). The open innovation research landscape: Established perspectives and emerging themes across different levels of analysis. *Industry and Innovation*, 24(1), 8–40. doi: 10.1080/13662716.2016.1240068

Borghys, K., van der Graaf, S., Walravens, N., & Van Compernolle, M. (2020). Multi-stakeholder innovation in smart city discourse: Quadruple helix thinking in the age of 'platforms.' *Frontiers in Sustainable Cities, 2.* doi: 10.3389/frsc.2020.00005

Bozeman, B. (2002). Public-value failure: When efficient markets may not do. *Public Administration Review, 62*(2), 145–61. doi: 10.1111/0033-3352.00165

Bozeman, B. (2007). *Public value and public interest: Counterbalancing economic individualism.* Washington, DC: Georgetown University Press.

Brandsen, T. (2021). Vulnerable citizens: Will co-production make a difference? In E. Loeffler & T. Bovaird (Eds.), *The Palgrave handbook of co-production of public services and outcomes* (pp. 527–539). Cham: Springer International Publishing.

Brandsen, T., Steen, T., & Verschuere, B. (Eds.) (2018). *Co-production and co-creation: Engaging citizens in public services.* New York, NY: Routledge.

Brenner, W., Uebernickel, F., & Abrell, T. (2016). Design thinking as mindset, process, and toolbox. In W. Brenner & F. Uebernickel (Eds.), *Design thinking for innovation: Research and practice* (pp. 3–21). Cham: Springer International Publishing.

Breuer, J., & Pierson, J. (2021). The right to the city and data protection for developing citizen-centric digital cities. *Information, Communication & Society, 24*(6), 797–812. doi: 10.1080/1369118X.2021.1909095

Breuer, J., Walravens, N., Van der Graaf, S., & Mariën, I. (2019). The right to the (smart) city, participation and open data. In S. M., Figueiredo, S., Krishnamurthy & T. Schröder (Eds.), *Architecture and the smart city* (pp. 126–136). New York, NY: Routledge.

Brewer, G. D. (1999). The challenges of interdisciplinarity. *Policy Sciences, 32*(4), 327–337.

Brill, M. (2019). Interactive democracy: New challenges for social choice theory. In J.-F. Laslier, H. Moulin, M. R. Sanver, & W. S. Zwicker (Eds.), *The future of economic design: The continuing development of a field as envisioned by its researchers, studies in economic design* (pp. 59–66). Cham: Springer International Publishing.

British Columbia. (n.d.). The service design playbook. Government Communications and Public Engagement.

Brown, T. (2008). Design thinking. *Harvard Business Review, 86*(6), 84.

Bruns, A. (2007). The future is user-led: The path towards widespread produsage. In Hutchinson, A (Ed.), *Proceedings of perthDAC 2007: The 7th International Digital Arts and Culture Conference*. Curtin University of Technology, Australia, Western Australia, Perth, pp. 68–77.

Bruns, A. (2008). The future is user-led: The path towards widespread produsage. *The Fibreculture Journal*, *11*(11), FCJ-066.

Bryson, J. M. (1995). *Strategic planning for public and nonprofit organizations: A guide to strengthening and sustaining organizational achievement*. Revised. San Francisco, CA: Jossey-Bass.

Bryson, J. M., & Bromiley, P. (1993). Critical factors affecting the planning and implementation of major projects. *Strategic Management Journal*, *14*(5), 319–337. doi: 10.1002/smj.4250140502

Bryson, J. M., Crosby, B. C., & Stone, M. M. (2015). Designing and implementing cross-sector collaborations: Needed and challenging. *Public Administration Review*, *75*(5), 647–663. doi: 10.1111/puar.12432

Bryson, J. M., Quick, K. S., Slotterback, C. S., & Crosby, B. C. (2013). Designing public participation processes. *Public Administration Review*, *73*(1), 23–34. doi: 10.1111/j.1540-6210.2012.02678.x

Bryson, J. M., Sancino, A., Benington, J., & Sørensen, E. (2017). Towards a multi-actor theory of public value co-creation. *Public Management Review*, *19*(5), 640–654. doi: 10.1080/14719037.2016.1192164

Budd, L., & Sancino, A. (2016). A framework for city leadership in multilevel governance settings: The comparative contexts of Italy and the UK. *Regional Studies, Regional Science*, *3*(1), 129–145. doi: 10.1080/21681376.2015.1125306

Buijs, A., Hansen, R., Van der Jagt, S., Ambrose-Oji, B., Elands, B., Lorance Rall, E., … Møller, M. S. (2019). Mosaic governance for urban green infrastructure: Upscaling active citizenship from a local government perspective. *Urban Forestry & Urban Greening*, *40*, 53–62. doi: 10.1016/j.ufug.2018.06.011

Burgess, J. E. (2007). *Vernacular creativity and new media*. PhD, Queensland University of Technology.

Bussu, S., & Bartels, K. P. R. (2014). Facilitative leadership and the challenge of renewing local democracy in Italy. *International Journal of Urban and Regional Research*, *38*(6), 2256–2273. doi: 10.1111/1468-2427.12070

Cameron, K., & Quinn, R. (2011). *Diagnosing and changing organizational culture: Based on the competing values framework* (3rd ed.). San Francisco, CA: Jossey-Bass.

Cammaerts, B. (2012). Protest logics and the mediation opportunity structure. *European Journal of Communication*, 27(2), 117–134. doi: 10.1177/0267323112441007

Cardullo, P., Di Feliciantonio, C., & Kitchin, R. (Eds.) (2019). *The right to the smart city*. Bingley: Emerald Publishing Limited.

Cardullo, P., Kitchin, R., & Di Feliciantonio, C. (2017). Living labs and vacancy in the neoliberal city. *Cities*, 73, 44–50.

Carlile, P. R. (2004). Transferring, translating, and transforming: An integrative framework for managing knowledge across boundaries. *Organization Science*, 15(5), 555–568. doi: 10.1287/orsc.1040.0094

Carpentier, N. (2016). Beyond the ladder of participation: An analytical toolkit for the critical analysis of participatory media processes. *Javnost – The Public*, 23(1), 70–88. doi: 10.1080/13183222.2016.1149760

Chesbrough, H. (2003). *Open innovation: The new imperative for creating and profiting from technology*. Boston, MA: Harvard Business Press.

Chesbrough, H. (2006). *Open business models: How to thrive in the new innovation landscape*. Boston, MA: Harvard Business Press.

Chesbrough, H., & Bogers, M. (2014). *Explicating open innovation: Clarifying an emerging paradigm for understanding innovation*. New Frontiers in Open Innovation (pp. 3–28). Oxford: Oxford University Press.

Chesbrough, H., Vanhaverbeke, W., & West, J. (Eds.) (2006). *Open innovation: Researching a new paradigm*. Oxford: Oxford University Press.

Cho, Y. J., & Poister, T. H. (2013). Human resource management practices and trust in public organizations. *Public Management Review*, 15(6), 816–838. doi: 10.1080/14719037.2012.698854

Cizek, K., & Uricchio, W. (2019). Introduction and overview. In *Collective wisdom* (1st ed.). Cambridge, MA: MIT Press. Retrieved from https://wip.mitpress.mit.edu/collectivewisdom

Claver-Cortés, E., Llopis, J., Gascó, J. L., Manchón, H. M., & Flor, F. J. C. (1999). Public administration: From bureaucratic culture to citizen-oriented culture. *International Journal of Public Sector Management*. doi: 10.1108/09513559910300226

Cluley, V., Parker, S., & Radnor, Z. (2020). New development: Expanding public service value to include dis/value. *Public Money & Management*, *0*(0), 1–4. doi: 10.1080/09540962.2020.1737392

Cluley, V., & Radnor, Z. (2020). Progressing the conceptualization of value co-creation in public service organizations. *Perspectives on Public Management and Governance*, *3*(3), 211–221. doi: 10.1093/ppmgov/gvz024

Cohen, J. E. (2019). Turning privacy inside out. *Theoretical Inquiries in Law*, *20*(1), 1–31. doi: 10.1515/til-2019-0002

Collins, A., Joseph, D., & Bielaczyc, K. (2004). Design research: Theoretical and methodological issues. *Journal of the Learning Sciences*, *13*(1), 15–42. doi: 10.1207/s15327809jls1301_2

Compagnucci, L., Spigarelli, F., Coelho, J., Duarte, C. (2021). Living Labs and user engagement for innovation and sustainability. *J. Clean. Prod. 289*, 125–721.

Costigan, R. D., Iiter, S. S., & Jason Berman, J. (1998). A multi-dimensional study of trust in organizations. *Journal of Managerial Issues*, *10*(3), 303–317.

Cottam, H., & Leadbeater, C. (2004). HEALTH: Co-creating services. *Design Council*, *57*.

Couldry, N., & Yu, J. (2018). Deconstructing datafication's brave new world. *New Media & Society*, *20*(12), 4473–4491. doi: 10.1177/1461444818775968

Cox, M. D., Green, L., Borodako, K., & Sangiorgi, D. (2015). Designing for public sector innovation in the UK: Design strategies for paradigm shifts. *Foresight*.

Daglio, M., Gerson, D., & Kitchen, H. (2014). Building organisational capacity for public sector innovation. Background Paper prepared for the OECD Conference Innovating the Public Sector: From Ideas to Impact, Paris, France.

Davies, A. J. (2019). Increasing the disaster resilience of remote communities through scenario co-creation.

De Koning, J., Crul, M., & Wever, R. (2016). Models of co-creation.

De Lange, M., & De Waal, M. (2019). *The hackable city: Digital media and collaborative city-making in the network society*. Singapore: Springer Nature.

de Waal, M., & Dignum, M. (2017). The citizen in the smart city. How the smart city could transform citizenship. *Inf. Technol.*, *59*, 263–273.

Deal, T. E., & Kennedy, A. A. (1982). *Corporate cultures: The rights and rituals of corporate life*. London: Addison-Wesley.

Deleuze, G., & Guattari, F. (1987). A thousand plateaus: Capitalism and schizophrenia, Trans. *Brian Massumi (London: Continuum, 2004)*, 322.

Denhardt, R. B., & Denhardt, J. V. (2000). The new public service: Serving rather than steering. *Public Administration Review, 60*(6), 549–559. doi: 10.1111/0033-3352.00117

Dobrigkeit, F., de Paula, D., & Uflacker, M. (2019). InnoDev: A software development methodology integrating design thinking, scrum and lean startup. In H. Plattner, C. Mienel & L. Leifer (Eds.) *Design thinking research* (pp. 199–227). Cham: Springer.

Dryzek, J. S. (2002). *Deliberative democracy and beyond: Liberals, critics, contestations*. Oxford: Oxford University Press.

Dubos, R. (2017). *Social capital: Theory and research*. Routledge.

Dudau, A., Glennon, R., & Verschuere, B. (2019). Following the Yellow Brick Road? (Dis)Enchantment with co-design, co-production and value co-creation in public services. *Public Management Review, 21*(11), 1577–1594. doi: 10.1080/14719037.2019.1653604

Dunleavy, P., Margetts, H., Bastow, S., & Tinkler, J. (2006). New public management is dead – Long live digital-era governance. *Journal of Public Administration Research and Theory, 16*(3), 467–494. doi: 10.1093/jopart/mui057

Eagan, J. L. (2017). Deliberative democracy. *Encyclopedia Britannica*.

Edelson, D. C. (2002). Design research: What we learn when we engage in design. *Journal of the Learning Sciences, 11*(1), 105–121. doi: 10.1207/S15327809JLS1101_4

Edvardsson, B., Gustafsson, A., Sandén, B., & Johnson, M. D. (2000). *New service development and innovation in the new economy*. Studenlitteratur.

Edwards, E. (1988). Corporate culture. *Management Accounting London, 66*(5), 18–20.

Edwards, L. (2016). Privacy, security and data protection in smart cities: A critical EU law perspective. *European Data Protection Law Review, 2*, 28.

Ehn, P. (2008). Participation in design things. In *Proceedings of the tenth anniversary conference on participatory design 2008, PDC '08* (pp. 92–101). USA: Indiana University.

Eizaguirre, S., Pradel-Miquel, M., & García, M. (2017). Citizenship practices and democratic governance: 'Barcelona En Comú' as an urban citizenship confluence promoting a new policy agenda. *Citizenship Studies, 21*(4), 425–439. doi: 10.1080/13621025.2017.1307609

Esposito, P., & Ricci, P. (2015). How to turn public (dis)value into new public value? Evidence from Italy. *Public Money & Management, 35*(3), 227–231. doi: 10.1080/09540962.2015.1027499

Etzkowitz, H., & Leydesdorff, L. (1995). *The Triple Helix – University-industry-government relations: A laboratory for knowledge based economic development.* SSRN Scholarly Paper. ID 2480085. Rochester, NY: Social Science Research Network.

Etzkowitz, H., & Leydesdorff, L. (2000). The dynamics of innovation: From National Systems and 'Mode 2' to a Triple Helix of university–industry–government relations. *Research Policy, 29*(2), 109–123.

European Commission. Joint Research Centre. (2016). *Citizen engagement in science and policy-making.* LU: Publications Office.

Ferlie, E., & Ongaro, E. (2015). *Strategic management in public services organizations: Concepts, schools and contemporary issues.* Abingdon: Routledge.

Fernandes, T., & Remelhe, P. (2016). How to engage customers in co-creation: Customers' motivations for collaborative innovation. *Journal of Strategic Marketing, 24*(3–4), 311–326. doi: 10.1080/0965254X.2015.1095220

Fledderus, J. (2018). The effects of co-production on trust. In *Co-production and co-creation.* Routledge.

Floridia, A. (2017). From participation to deliberation: A critical genealogy of deliberative democracy.

Foray, D. (2004). *Economics of knowledge.* Cambridge, MA: MIT Press.

Foth, M., Tomitsch, M., Satchell, C., & Hank Haeusler, M. (2015). From users to citizens: Some thoughts on designing for polity and civics. In *Proceedings of the annual meeting of the Australian special interest group for computer human interaction, OzCHI '15* (pp. 623–633). New York, NY: Association for Computing Machinery.

Freeman, R. E. (1984). *Strategic management: A stakeholder approach*. Boston, MA: Pitman.

Freeman, R. E. (2010). *Strategic management: A stakeholder approach*. Cambridge: Cambridge University Press.

Fung, A. (2006). Varieties of participation in complex governance. *Public Administration Review*, 66(s1), 66–75. doi: 10.1111/j.1540-6210. 2006.00667.x

Fung, A. (2015). Putting the public back into governance: The challenges of citizen participation and its future. *Public Administration Review*, 75(4), 513–522. doi: 10.1111/puar.12361

Gambi, L. D. N., Boer, H., Gerolamo, M. C., Jørgensen, F., & Carpinetti, L. C. R. (2015). The relationship between organizational culture and quality techniques, and its impact on operational performance. *International Journal of Operations & Production Management*, 35(10), 1460–1484. doi: 10.1108/IJOPM-12-2013-0563

Geels, F. W., & Schot, J. (2010). The dynamics of transitions: A socio-technical perspective. *Transitions to Sustainable Development: New Directions in the Study of Long Term Transformative Change*, 11–104.

Genc, E. (2017). *Strategy implementation, organizational culture and performance in Turkish Local Government*. PhD, Cardiff University, Cardiff.

George, B., Desmidt, S., Cools, E., & Prinzie, A. (2018). Cognitive styles, user acceptance and commitment to strategic plans in public organizations: An empirical analysis. *Public Management Review*, 20(3), 340–359. doi: 10.1080/14719037.2017.1285112

Godinho, M. A., Borda, A., Kariotis, T., Molnar, A., Kostkova, P., & Liaw, S.-T. (2021). Knowledge co-creation in participatory policy and practice: Building community through data-driven direct democracy. *Big Data & Society*, 8(1), 20539517211019430. doi: 10.1177/20539517211019430

Goh, J. M., & Arenas, A. E. (2020). IT value creation in public sector: How IT-enabled capabilities mitigate tradeoffs in public organisations. *European Journal of Information Systems*, 29(1), 25–43. doi: 10.1080/0960085X.2019.1708821

Gottlieb, M., Wagner, E., Wagner, A., & Chan, T. (2017). Applying design thinking principles to curricular development in medical education. *AEM Education and Training*, 1(1), 21–26. doi: 10.1002/aet2.10003

Graham, M., Kitchin, R., Mattern, S., & Shaw, J. (2019). *How to run a city like Amazon, and Other Fables*. London: Meatspace Press.

Grant, R. (1999). The resource-based theory of competitive advantage: Implications for strategy formulation. *California Management Review, 33,* 3–23. doi: 10.1016/B978-0-7506-7088-3.50004-8

Grindle, M. (2010). Good Governance: The Inflation of an Idea. *Harvard Kennedy School,* 21.

Grönroos, C. (2011). Value co-creation in service logic: A critical analysis. *Marketing Theory, 11*(3), 279–301. doi: 10.1177/1470593111408177

Guillot, L., & Schaart, E. (2021). Court finds brussels not doing enough to fight air pollution. *POLITICO.* Retrieved from https://www.politico.eu/article/court-finds-brussels-regional-government-not-doing-enough-to-fight-air-pollution/. Accessed on June 16, 2021.

Gyrd-Jones, R. I., & Kornum, N. (2013). Managing the co-created brand: Value and cultural complementarity in online and offline multi-stakeholder ecosystems. *Journal of Business Research, 66*(9), 1484–1493. doi: 10.1016/j.jbusres.2012.02.045

Habermas, J. (1981). *Theorie des kommunikativen Handelns. Buch von Jürgen Habermas (Suhrkamp Verlag).* Frankfurt am Main: Suhrkamp Verlag.

Hambeukers, D. (2019). The new double diamond design process is here. *Medium.* Retrieved from https://medium.com/design-leadership-notebook/the-new-double-diamond-design-process-7c8f12d7945e. Accessed on June 22, 2021.

Hambleton, R., & Howard, J. (2013). Place-based leadership and public service innovation. *Local Government Studies, 39*(1), 47–70. doi: 10.1080/03003930.2012.693076

Hansen, A. V., & Fuglsang, L. (2020). Living labs as an innovation tool for public value creation: Possibilities and pitfalls. *Innovation Journal, 25*(3), 4.

Hartley, J. (2005). Innovation in governance and public services: Past and present. *Public Money & Management, 25*(1), 27–34. doi: 10.1111/j.1467-9302.2005.00447.x

Hartley, J., Parker, S., & Beashel, J. (2019). Leading and recognizing public value. *Public Administration, 97*(2), 264–278. doi: 10.1111/padm.12563

Harvey, D. (2003). The right to the city. *International Journal of Urban and Regional Research, 27*(4), 939–941.

Hasche, N., Höglund, L., & Mårtensson, M. (2020). Intra-organizational trust in public organizations – The study of interpersonal trust in both vertical and horizontal relationships from a bidirectional perspective. *Public Management Review*, *0*(0), 1–21. doi: 10.1080/14719037.2020.1764081

Hatch, M. J., & Cunliffe, A. L. (2006). *Organizational theory* (2nd ed.). Oxford: Oxford University Press.

Hatuka, T., Rosen-Zvi, I., Birnhack, M., Toch, E., & Zur, H. (2018). The political premises of contemporary urban concepts: The global city, the sustainable city, the resilient city, the creative city, and the smart city. *Planning Theory & Practice*, *19*(2), 160–179. doi: 10.1080/14649357. 2018.1455216

Head, B. W., & Alford, J. (2015). Wicked problems: Implications for public policy and management. *Administration & Society*, *47*(6), 711–739. doi: 10.1177/0095399713481601

Heikkila, T., & Gerlak, A. K. (2013). Building a conceptual approach to collective learning: Lessons for public policy scholars. *Policy Studies Journal*, *41*(3), 484–512. doi: 10.1111/psj.12026

Heritage, B., Pollock, C., & Roberts, L. (2014). Validation of the organizational culture assessment instrument. *PloS One*, *9*(3), e92879. doi: 10.1371/journal.pone.0092879

Hess, M., & Adams, D. (2007). Innovation in public management: The role and function of community knowledge. *The Innovation Journal: The Public Sector Innovation Journal*, *12*(1), 1–20.

Hilgers, D., & Ihl, C. (2010). Citizensourcing: Applying the concept of open innovation to the public sector. *The International Journal of Public Participation*, *4*(1), 67–88.

Hofstede, G. (2001). *Culture's consequences: Comparing values, behaviors, institutions, and organizations across nations*. Thousand Oaks, CA: Sage.

Hofstede, G., Neuijen, B., Ohayv, D. D., & Sanders, G. (1990). Measuring organizational cultures: A qualitative and quantitative study across twenty cases. *Administrative Science Quarterly*, *35*(2), 286–316. doi: 10.2307/ 2393392

Höglund, L., & Mårtensson, M. (2019). Entrepreneurship as a strategic management tool for renewal: The case of the Swedish Public Employment Service. *Administrative Sciences*, *9*(4), 76. doi: 10.3390/admsci9040076

Holm, F., & Berardo, R. (2020). Coalitional architecture of climate change litigation networks in the United States. *Review of Policy Research*, *37*(6), 797–822. doi: 10.1111/ropr.12402

Hölscher, K., & Frantzeskaki, N. (2021). Perspectives on urban transformation research: Transformations in, of, and by cities. *Urban Transformations*, *3*(1), 2. doi: 10.1186/s42854-021-00019-z

Homburg, C., & Jensen, O. (2007). The thought worlds of marketing and sales: Which differences make a difference? *Journal of Marketing*, *71*(3), 124–142.

Hood, C. (1991). A public management for all seasons? *Public Administration*, *69*(1), 3–19. doi: 10.1111/j.1467-9299.1991.tb00779.x

Hossain, M., Leminen, S., & Westerlund, M. (2019). A systematic review of living lab literature. *Journal of Cleaner Production*, *213*:976–88. doi: 10.1016/j.jclepro.2018.12.257

Hupe, P. L., & Hill, M. J. (2016). 'And the Rest Is Implementation.' Comparing approaches to what happens in policy processes beyond great expectations. *Public Policy and Administration*, *31*(2), 103–121. doi: 10.1177/0952076715598828

Husk, S. (2018). Creating a culture of risk taking and experimentation | Planbox (Formerly Imaginatik). Retrieved from https://www.imaginatik.com/creating-a-culture-of-risk-taking-and-experimentation/. Accessed on July 3, 2021.

Huybrechts, L., Benesch, H., & Geib, J. (2017). Institutioning: Participatory design, co-design and the public realm. *CoDesign*, *13*(3), 148–159. doi: 10.1080/15710882.2017.1355006

Innes, J., & Booher, D. (2018). *Planning with complexity: An introduction to collaborative rationality for public policy* (2nd ed.). New York, NY: Routledge.

Irvin, R. A., & Stansbury, J. (2004). Citizen participation in decision making: Is it worth the effort? *Public Administration Review*, *64*(1), 55–65. doi: 10.1111/j.1540-6210.2004.00346.x

Jaques, E. (1951). *The changing culture of a factory*. London: Routledge.

Järvi, H., Kähkönen, A.-K., & Torvinen, H. (2018). When value co-creation fails: Reasons that lead to value co-destruction. *Scandinavian Journal of Management*, *34*(1), 63–77. doi: 10.1016/j.scaman.2018.01.002

Jenkins, H. (2006). *Convergence culture*. New York, NY: New York University Press.

Jørgensen, T. B., & Bozeman, B. (2007). Public values: An inventory. *Administration & Society, 39*(3), 354–381. doi: 10.1177/0095399707300703

Kaplan, R. S., Norton, D. P., & Inc Books24x7. (2004). *Strategy maps [Electronic Resource]: Converting intangible assets into tangible outcomes*. Boston, MA: Harvard Business School Press.

Karwan, K. R., & Markland, R. E. (2006). Integrating service design principles and information technology to improve delivery and productivity in public sector operations: The case of the South Carolina DMV. *Journal of Operations Management, 24*(4), 347–362. doi: 10.1016/j.jom.2005.06.003

Kassim, H., & Le Galès, P. (2010). Exploring governance in a multi-level polity: A policy instruments approach. *West European Politics, 33*(1), 1–21.

Kieliszewski, C. A., Maglio, P. P., & Cefkin, M. (2012). On modeling value constellations to understand complex service system interactions. *European Management Journal, 30*(5), 438–450.

Kirchgeorg, M., Meynhardt, T., Pinkwart, A., Suchanek, A., & Zülch, H. (2017). *Das Leipziger Führungsmodell: The Leipzig Leadership Model*. BoD–Books on Demand.

Kitchin, R. (2021). *Decentering the smart city*.

Kitchin, R., Cardullo, P., & Feliciantonio, C. D. (2018). *Citizenship, justice and the right to the smart city*.

Kitchin, R., Cardullo, P., & Feliciantonio, C. D. (2019). Citizenship, justice, and the right to the smart city. In P. Cardullo, C. D. Feliciantonio, & R. Kitchin (Eds.), *The right to the smart city* (pp. 1–24). Bingley: Emerald Publishing Limited.

Kitchin, R., & Dodge, M. (2011). *Code/Space: Software and everyday life*. Cambridge, MA: MIT Press.

Komninos, N., & Mora, L. (2018). Exploring the big picture of smart city research. *Scienze Regionali-The Italian Journal of Regional Science, 1*, 15–38.

Koster, M. (2014). Bridging the Cap in the Dutch Participation Society: New spaces of governance, brokers, and informal politics. *Etnofoor, 26*(2), 49–64.

Kotter, J. P. (2008). *Corporate culture and performance*. New York, NY: Simon and Schuster.

Krippendorff, K. (1989). On the essential contexts of artifacts or on the proposition that design is making sense (of Things). *Design Issues, 5*(2), 9–39.

Kurniawan, S. (2004). Interaction design: Beyond human–computer interaction by Preece, Sharp and Rogers (2001), ISBN 0471492787. *Universal Access in the Information Society, 3*(3), 289–289.

Laenens, W., Mariën, I., & Walravens, N. (2019). Participatory action research for the development of e-inclusive smart cities. *Architecture and Culture, 7*(3), 457–471. doi: 10.1080/20507828.2019.1679447

Lan, Z., & Rosenbloom, D. H. (1992). Editorial: Public administration in transition? *Public Administration Review, 52*(6), 535–537. doi: 10.2307/977163

Larsson, O. (2019). A theoretical framework for analyzing institutionalized domination in network governance arrangements. *Critical Policy Studies, 13*(1), 81–100. doi: 10.1080/19460171.2017.1393440

Leadbeater, C. (2004). *Personalisation through participation: A new script for public services*. London: Demos.

Leadbeater, C., & Miller, P. (2004). *The pro-am revolution: How enthusiasts are changing our society and economy*. London: Demos.

Lee, A., Mackenzie, A., Smith, G. J. D., & Box, P. (2020). Mapping platform urbanism: Charting the nuance of the platform pivot. *Urban Planning, 5*(1), 116–128. doi: 10.17645/up.v5i1.2545

Lefebvre, H. (1968). *Le Droit à La Ville*. Seuil: S.L.

Lefebvre, H., Kofman, E., & Lebas, E. (1996). *Writings on cities* (Vol. 63). Oxford: Blackwell.

Leino, H., & Puumala, E. (2020). What can co-creation do for the citizens? Applying co-creation for the promotion of participation in cities. *Environment and Planning C: Politics and Space*, 239965442095733. doi: 10.1177/2399654420957337

Leino, H., & Puumala, E. (2021). What can co-creation do for the citizens? Applying co-creation for the promotion of participation in cities. *Environment and Planning C: Politics and Space, 39*(4), 781–799. doi: 10.1177/2399654420957337

Lember, V., Brandsen, T., & Tõnurist, P. (2019). The potential impacts of digital technologies on co-production and co-creation. *Public Management Review, 21*(11), 1665–1686. doi: 10.1080/14719037.2019.1619807

Leticia Santos-Vijande, M., González-Mieres, C., & Ángel López-Sánchez, J. (2013). An assessment of innovativeness in KIBS: Implications on KIBS' co-creation culture, innovation capability, and performance. *Journal of Business & Industrial Marketing, 28*(2), 86–102. doi: 10.1108/08858621311295236

Levy, P. (2015). Collective intelligence for educators. *Educational Philosophy and Theory, 47*(8), 749–754. doi: 10.1080/00131857.2015.1053734

Lindblom, C. E. (1959). The science of 'muddling through.' *Public Administration Review, 19*(2), 79–88. doi: 10.2307/973677

Litcanu, M., Prostean, O., Oros, C., & Mnerie, A. V. (2015). Brain-writing vs. brainstorming case study for power engineering education. *Procedia – Social and Behavioral Sciences, 191*, 387–390. doi: 10.1016/j.sbspro.2015.04.452

Livingstone, S. (2003). The changing nature of audiences: From the mass audience to the interactive media user. In A. Valdivia (Ed.), *Companion to media studies* (pp. 337–359). Oxford: Blackwell Publishing.

Livingstone, S. (2013). The participation paradigm in audience research. *The Communication Review, 16*(1–2), 21–30. doi: 10.1080/10714421.2013.757174

Livingstone, S. (2019). Audiences in an age of datafication: Critical questions for media research. *Television & New Media, 20*(2), 170–183. doi: 10.1177/1527476418811118

Loideain, N. N. (2019). A port in the data-sharing storm: The GDPR and the Internet of Things. *Journal of Cyber Policy, 4*(2), 178–196. doi: 10.1080/23738871.2019.1635176

Lund, D. H. (2018). Co-creation in urban governance: From inclusion to innovation. *Scandinavian Journal of Public Administration, 22*(2), 3–17.

Lupton, D. (2018). How do data come to matter? Living and becoming with personal data. *Big Data & Society, 5*(2), 2053951718786314. doi: 10.1177/2053951718786314

MacCarthaigh, M. (2008). *Public service values.* Committee for Public Management Research Discussion Paper. 39. Dublin: Institute of Public Administration.

Malmberg, K., Vaittinen, I., Evans, P., Schuurman, D., Ståhlbröst, A., & Vervoort, K. (2017). *Living lab methodology handbook.* doi: 10.5281/ZENODO.1146321

Malmberg, L., & Wetter-Edman, K. (2016). Design in public sector: Exploring antecedents of sustained design capability. In *20th DMI: Academic design management conference-inflection point: Design research meets design practice, Boston, USA, July 22–29, 2016* (pp. 1287–1307). Design Management Institute.

March, J. G., & Olsen, J. (2008). The logic of appropriateness. In R. E. Goodin, M. Moran & M. Rein (Eds.), *The Oxford handbook of public policy* (p. 689). Oxford: Oxford University Press.

March, J. G., & Olsen, J. P. (2011). The logic of appropriateness. *The Oxford handbook of political science*. Retrieved from https://www.oxfordhandbooks.com/view/10.1093/oxfordhb/9780199604456.001.0001/oxfordhb-9780199604456-e-024. Accessed on May 19, 2021.

Marsh, S. L. (2007). *Using and evaluating HCI techniques in geovisualization: Applying standard and adapted methods in research and education.* Unpublished Phd D thesis, City University, London.

Martin, B., Hanington, B., & Hanington, B. M. (2012). *Universal methods of design: 100 ways to research complex problems, develop innovative ideas, and design effective solutions.* Rockport Publishers.

Mattelmäki, T., & Sleeswijk-Visser, F. (2011). Lost in CO-X – Interpretations of co-design and co-creation. In L.-L. C. Norbert Roozenburg (Ed.), *Proceedings of IASDR'11, 4th World Conference on Design Research, Delft University.*

Mazzocchi, F. (2019). Scientific research across and beyond disciplines. *EMBO Reports, 20*(6), e47682. doi: 10.15252/embr.201947682

Mazzucato, M. (2021). *Mission economy: A moonshot guide to changing capitalism.* London: Allen Lane.

Mazzucato, M., & Ryan-Collins, J. (2019). Putting value creation back into 'Public Value': From market-fixing to market-shaping. *UCL Institute for Innovation and Public Purpose, University College London.* Retrieved from https://www.ucl.ac.uk/bartlett/public-purpose/publications/2019/jun/putting-value-creation-back-public-value-market-fixing-market-shaping. Accessed on March 29, 2021.

Meijer, A. (2012). Co-production in an information age: Individual and community engagement supported by new media. *VOLUNTAS: International Journal of Voluntary and Nonprofit Organizations, 23*(4), 1156–1172.

Menguc, B., & Auh, S. (2006). Creating a firm-level dynamic capability through capitalizing on market orientation and innovativeness. *Journal of the Academy of Marketing Science*, 34(1), 63–73. doi: 10.1177/0092070305281090

Meynhardt, T. (2009). Public value inside: What is public value creation? *International Journal of Public Administration*, 32(3–4), 192–219. doi: 10.1080/01900690902732632

Meynhardt, T. (2015). Public value: Turning a conceptual framework into a scorecard. In J. Bryson, B. Crosby, & L. Bloomberg (Eds.), *Public value and public administration* (pp. 147–169). Washington, DC: Georgetown University Press.

Michels, A. (2011). Innovations in democratic governance-how does citizen participation contribute to a better democracy? *International Review of Administrative Sciences*, 77, 275–293. doi: 10.1177/0020852311399851

Mintzberg, H., Ahlstrand, B. W., & Lampel, J. (1998). *Strategy Safari: A guided tour through the wilds of strategic management*. New York, NY: Free Press.

Mitchell, D. (2003). *The right to the city: Social justice and the fight for public space*. New York, NY: Guilford Press.

Mogstad, A., Høiseth, M., & Pettersen, I. N. (2018). Co-creation in public service innovation: A review of how to encourage employee engagement in co-creation. *DS 91: Proceedings of NordDesign 2018, Linköping, Sweden*, 14th–17th August 2018.

Moore, M. H. (1995). *Creating public value: Strategic management in government*. Boston, MA: Harvard University Press.

Moore, M. H. (2013). *Recognizing public value*. Boston, MA: Harvard University Press.

Morozov, E., & Bria, F. (2018). *Democratizing urban technology*. New York, NY: Rosa Luxemburg Foundation.

Morrow, J. L., Hansen, M. H., & Pearson, A. W. (2004). The cognitive and affective antecedents of general trust within cooperative organizations. *Journal of Managerial Issues*, 16(1), 48–64.

Mosco, V. (2019). *The smart city in a digital world*. Bingley: Emerald Publishing Limited.

Moynihan, D. P., & Pandey, S. K. (2010). The big question for performance management: Why do managers use performance information? *Journal of*

Public Administration Research and Theory, 20(4), 849–866. doi: 10.1093/jopart/muq004

Mulgan, G. (2006). The process of social innovation. *Innovations: Technology, Governance, Globalization, 1*(2), 145–162. doi: 10.1162/itgg.2006.1.2.145

Mulgan, G., & Albury, D. (2003). Innovation in the public sector. *Strategy Unit, Cabinet Office, 1*(1), 40.

Mulgan, G., Tucker, S., Ali, R., & Sanders, B. (2007). *Social innovation: What it is, why it matters, how it can be accelerated.*

Murray-Webster, R., & Simon, P. (2006). Making sense of stakeholder mapping. *PM World Today, 8*(11), 1–4.

Nabatchi, T., Sancino, A., & Sicilia, M. (2017). Varieties of participation in public services: The who, when, and what of coproduction. *Public Administration Review, 77*(5), 766–776. doi: 10.1111/puar.12765

Nail, T. (2017). What is an assemblage? *Substance, 46*(1), 21–37. doi: 10.3368/ss.46.1.21

Nambisan, S., & Nambisan, P. (2013). *Engaging citizens in co-creation in public services: Lessons learned and best practices.* IBM Center for the Business of Government – Collaboration Across Boundaries Series.

Neblo, M. A., Esterling, K. M., & Lazer, D. M. J. (2018). *Politics with the people: Building a directly representative democracy.*

Nederhand, J., & van Meerkerk, I. (2017). Activating Citizens in Dutch Care Reforms: Framing new co-production roles and competences for citizens and professionals. *Policy and Politics, 46*(4), 533–550. doi: 10.1332/030557317 X15035697297906

Neumeier, S. (2017). Social innovation in rural development: Identifying the key factors of success. *The Geographical Journal, 183*(1), 34–46. doi: 10.1111/geoj.12180

Nguyen Long, L. A., Foster, M., & Arnold, G. (2019). The impact of stakeholder engagement on local policy decision making. *Policy Sciences, 52*(4), 549–571. doi: 10.1007/s11077-019-09357-z

Nica, E. (2013). Organizational culture in the public sector. *Economic, Management, and Financial Market, 8*(2), 179–184.

Niskanen, W. A. (1971). *Bureaucracy and representative government.* Chicago, IL: Aldine, Atherton.

Nitzl, C., Sicilia, M. F., & Steccolini, I. (2019). Exploring the links between different performance information uses, NPM cultural orientation, and organizational performance in the public sector. *Public Management Review*, *21*(5), 686–710. doi: 10.1080/14719037.2018.1508609

Noveck, B. S. (2015). *Smart citizens, smarter state: The technologies of expertise and the future of governing*. Cambridge, MA: Harvard University Press.

Oborn, E., & Dawson, S. (2010). Learning across communities of practice: An examination of multidisciplinary work. *British Journal of Management*, *21*(4), 843–858. doi: 10.1111/j.1467-8551.2009.00684.x

Ocnarescu, I., Pain, F., Bouchard, C., Aoussat, A., & Sciamma, D. (2011). Improvement of the industrial design process by the creation and usage of intermediate representations of technology, 'TechCards.' P. 1 in *Proceedings of the 2011 Conference on Designing Pleasurable Products and Interfaces - DPPI '11*. Milano: ACM Press.

OECD. (2019). *Public value in public service transformation.*

O'Flynn, J. (2021). Where to for public value? Taking stock and moving on. *International Journal of Public Administration*, *44*(10), 867–877. doi: 10.1080/01900692.2021.1884696

Oliveira, Á., & Campolargo, M. (2015). From smart cities to human smart cities. In 2015 *48th Hawaii international conference on system sciences* (pp. 2336–2344).

O'Riordan, J. (2015). *Organisational Culture and the Public Service, IPA State of the Public Service Series*. 16. IPA an Foras Riaracháin Institute Of Public Administration.

Osborne, D., & Gaebler, T. (1992). *Reinventing government: How the entrepreneurial spirit is transforming the public sector*. Reading, MA: Addison-Wesley.

Osborne, S. P. (2006). The new public governance? *Public Management Review*, *8*(3), 377–387. doi: 10.1080/14719030600853022

Osborne, S. P. (2018). From public service-dominant logic to public service logic: Are public service organizations capable of co-production and value co-creation? *Public Management Review*, *20*(2), 225–231. doi: 10.1080/14719037.2017.1350461

Osborne, S. P., Radnor, Z., Kinder, T., & Vidal, I. (2015). The SERVICE Framework: A public-service-dominant approach to sustainable public services. *British Journal of Management*, *26*(3), 424–438. doi: 10.1111/1467-8551.12094

Osborne, S. P., & Strokosch, K. (2013). It takes two to tango? Understanding the co-production of public services by integrating the services management and public administration perspectives. *British Journal of Management*, *24*(S1), S31–S47. doi: 10.1111/1467-8551.12010

Ostrom, A. L., Parasuraman, A., Bowen, D. E., Patrício, L., & Voss, C. A. (2015). Service research priorities in a rapidly changing context. *Journal of Service Research*, *18*(2), 127–159. https://doi.org/10.1177/1094670515576315

Ostrom, E. (1972). Metropolitan reform: Propositions derived from two traditions. *Social Science Quarterly*, *53*(3), 474–493.

Pahl, G., Beitz, W., Feldhusen, J., & Grote, K. (2007). *Engineering design: A systematic approach* (3rd ed., p. 632). Berlin: Springer Science+ Business Media Deutschland GmbH.

Parker, G., Van Alstyne, M., & Choudary, S. P. (2017). *Platform revolution: How networked markets are transforming the economy and how to make them work for you*. New York, NY: W.W. Norton & Company.

Parker, R., & Bradley, L. (2000). Organisational culture in the public sector: Evidence from six organisations. *International Journal of Public Sector Management*, *13*(2), 125–141. doi: 10.1108/09513550010338773

Patrício, L., Pinho, N., Teixeira, J., & Fisk, R. (2018). Service design for value networks: Enabling value cocreation interactions in healthcare. *Service Science*, *10*, 76–97. https://doi.org/10.1287/serv.2017.0201.

Payne, A. F., Storbacka, K., & Frow, P. (2008). Managing the co-creation of value. *Journal of the Academy of Marketing Science*, *36*(1), 83–96. doi: 10.1007/s11747-007-0070-0

Peña Gangadharan, S., & Niklas, J. (2019). Decentering technology in discourse on discrimination. *Information, Communication & Society*, *22*(7), 882–899.

Pettigrew, A. M., Thomas, H., & Whittington, R. (2002). *Handbook of strategy and management*. London: Sage Publications.

Pollit, C. (1990). *Managerialism and the public services: The Anglo-American experience*. Oxford: Blackwell.

Pollitt, C., & Bouckaert, G. (2017). *Public management reform: A comparative analysis – Into the age of austerity* (4th ed.). Oxford: Oxford University Press.

Porter, M. E. (1980). *Competitive strategy: Techniques for analyzing industries and competitors*. New York, NY: Free Press.

Prahalad, C. K., & Ramaswamy, V. (2000). Co-opting customer competence. *Harvard Business Review*, 78(1), 79–87.

Prahalad, C. K., & Ramaswamy, V. (2004). Co-creation experiences: The next practice in value creation. *Journal of Interactive Marketing*, 18(3), 5–14. doi: 10.1002/dir.20015

Pruitt, J., & Adlin, T. (2006). *The persona lifecycle: Keeping people in mind throughout product design*. Amsterdam: Elsevier: Morgan Kaufmann Publishers, an imprint of Elsevier.

Purcell, M. (2002). Excavating Lefebvre: The right to the city and its urban politics of the inhabitant. *GeoJournal*, 58(2), 99–108. doi: 10.1023/B:GEJO.0000010829.62237.8f

Quick, K., & Feldman, M. (2011). Distinguishing participation and inclusion. *Journal of Planning Education and Research*, 31, 272–290. doi: 10.1177/0739456X11410979

Quinn, R. E., & Rohrbaugh, J. (1983). A spatial model of effectiveness criteria: Towards a competing values approach to organizational analysis. *Management Science*, 29(3), 363–377.

Radnor, Z., Osborne, S. P., Kinder, T., & Mutton, J. (2014). Operationalizing co-production in public services delivery: The contribution of service blueprinting. *Public Management Review*, 16(3), 402–423. doi: 10.1080/14719037.2013.848923

Rainey, H. (2014). *Understanding and managing public organizations* (5th ed.). Hoboken, NJ: Jossey-Bass.

Ramaswamy, V., & Ozcan, K. (2018). What is co-creation? An interactional creation framework and its implications for value creation. *Journal of Business Research*, 84, 196–205. doi: 10.1016/j.jbusres.2017.11.027

Rao, M. (2021). Communities of innovation: From co-creation to resilience. *COMMUNITIES OF INNOVATION: How Organizations Harness Collective Creativity and Build Resilience*, 297–325.

Raymond, E. (1999). The cathedral and the bazaar. *Knowledge, Technology & Policy*, 12(3), 23–49. doi: 10.1007/s12130-999-1026-0

Redlich, T., Krenz, P., Basmer, S.-V., Buxbaum-Conradi, S., Wulf, S., & Wulfsberg, J. P. (2014). The impact of openness on value co-creation in production networks. *Procedia CIRP*, *16*, 44–49. doi: 10.1016/j.procir.2014.01.007

Rehman, S. (2019). *The mediating role of organizational capabilities between organizational performance and its determinants*, 23.

Reypens, C., Lievens, A., & Blazevic, V. (2021). Hybrid orchestration in multi-stakeholder innovation networks: Practices of mobilizing multiple, diverse stakeholders across organizational boundaries. *Organization Studies*, *42*(1), 61–83. doi: 10.1177/0170840619868268

Ritzer, G., & Jurgenson, N. (2010). Production, consumption, prosumption: The nature of capitalism in the age of the digital 'prosumer.' *Journal of Consumer Culture*, *10*(1), 13–36. doi: 10.1177/1469540509354673

Robbins, S. P. (2005). *Organizational behavior*. Englewood Cliffs, NJ: Prentice Hall International.

Roloff, J. (2008). Learning from multi-stakeholder networks: Issue-focussed stakeholder management. *Journal of Business Ethics*, *82*(1), 233–250. doi: 10.1007/s10551-007-9573-3

Rong, T., & Hongwei, S. (2012). Transformations of organizational culture in the public sector. *Cross-Cultural Communication*, *8*(4), 46–52.

Rosanvallon, P. (2011). *Democratic legitimacy: Impartiality, reflexivity, proximity*. Princeton, NJ: Princeton University Press.

Rösler, J., Söll, T., Hancock, L., & Friedli, T. (2021). Value co-creation between public service organizations and the private sector: An organizational capabilities perspective. *Administrative Sciences*, *11*(2). doi: 10.3390/admsci11020055

Rossi, P., & Tuurnas, S. (2021). Conflicts fostering understanding of value co-creation and service systems transformation in complex public service systems. *Public Management Review*, *23*(2), 254–275. doi: 10.1080/14719037.2019.1679231

Schaffers, H., García Guzmán, J., & Merz, C. (2010). Living labs for enhancing innovation and rural development: Methodology and implementation In H. Schaffers, J. García Guzmán, M. de la Cruz & C. Merz. *Living labs for rural development* (pp. 25–51). Madrid: Tragsa.

Scharpf, F. W. (2015). Political legitimacy in a non-optimal currency area. *Democratic Politics in a European Union under Stress*, 19–47.

Schein, E. H. (2004). *Organizational culture and leadership*. Hoboken, NJ: John Wiley & Sons.

Schmidt, V. A. (2013). Democracy and legitimacy in the European Union revisited: Input, output and 'throughput.' *Political Studies*, 61(1), 2–22.

Schmidthuber, L., & Hilgers, D. (2018). unleashing innovation beyond organizational boundaries: Exploring citizensourcing projects. *International Journal of Public Administration*, 41(4), 268–283. doi: 10.1080/01900692.2016.1263656

Schneider, B., & Barbera, K. M. (2014). Introduction: The Oxford handbook of organizational climate and culture. In B. Schneider & K. M. Barbera (Eds.), *The Oxford handbook of organizational climate and culture* (pp. 3–20). Oxford University Press. https://doi.org/10.1093/oxfordhb/9780199860715.013.0001.

Schneider, J., & Stickdorn, M. (2011). *This is service design thinking: Basics, tools, cases*. Hoboken, NJ: Wiley.

Schuurman, D., Baccarne, B., De Marez, L., Veeckman, C., & Ballon, P. (2016). Living Labs as open innovation systems for knowledge exchange: solutions for sustainable innovation development. *International Journal of Business Innovation and Research*, 10(2–3), 322–340. https://doi.org/10.1504/IJBIR.2016.074832

Scott, I., & Gong, T. (2021). Coordinating government silos: challenges and opportunities. *GPPG 1*, 20–38. https://doi.org/10.1007/s43508-021-00004-z, Belgium. https://publica.fraunhofer.de/eprints/urn_nbn_de_0011-n-534927-16.pdf

Secomandi, F., & Snelders, D. (2011). The object of service design. *Design Issues*, 27(3), 20–34.

Selden, L., & MacMillan, I. C. (2006). Manage customer-centric innovation-systematically. *Harvard Business Review*, 84(4), 108.

Shamim, A., Ghazali, Z., & Albinsson, P. A. (2017). Construction and validation of customer value co-creation attitude scale. *Journal of Consumer Marketing*, 34(7), 591–602. doi: 10.1108/JCM-01-2016-1664

Shin, S.-Y., Kim, D., & Chun, S. A. (2021). Digital divide in advanced smart city innovations. *Sustainability*, 13(7), 4076. doi: 10.3390/su13074076

Shostack, G. L. (1982). How to design a service. *European Journal of Marketing*, 16(1), 49–63.

Simon, H. A., & Barnard, C. I. (1947). *Administrative behavior: A study of decision-making processes in administrative organization*. New York, NY: Macmillan Co.

Slocum, N., & Steyaert, S. (2003). *Participatory methods toolkit: A practitioner's manual*. King Baudouin Foundation.

Snyder, C. (2003). *Paper prototyping: The fast and easy way to design and refine user interfaces*. Morgan Kaufmann.

Snyder, C. R., & Lopez, S. J. (2009). *Oxford handbook of positive psychology*. Oxford: Oxford University Press.

Solman, H., Smits, M., van Vliet, B., & Bush, S. (2021). Co-Production in the wind energy sector: A systematic literature review of public engagement beyond invited stakeholder participation. *Energy Research & Social Science*, 72, 101876. doi: 10.1016/j.erss.2020.101876

Sørensen, E., & Bentzen, T. (2020). Public administrators in interactive democracy: A multi-paradigmatic approach. *Local Government Studies*, 46(1), 139–162. doi: 10.1080/03003930.2019.1627335

Sørensen, E., & Torfing, J. (2011). Enhancing collaborative innovation in the public sector. *Administration & Society*, 43(8), 842–868. doi: 10.1177/0095399711418768

Sørensen, E., & Torfing, J. (2017). Metagoverning collaborative innovation in governance networks. *The American Review of Public Administration*, 47(7), 826–839. doi: 10.1177/0275074016643181

Sorensen, J. B. (2002). The strength of corporate culture and the reliability of firm performance. *Administrative Science Quarterly*, 47, 70–91.

Spagnoli, F., van der Graaf, S., & Brynskov, M. (2019). The paradigm shift of living labs in service co-creation for smart cities: SynchroniCity validation. In *Organizing for digital innovation* (pp. 135–147). Cham: Springer.

Steen, K., & van Bueren, E. (2017). The defining characteristics of urban living labs. *Technology Innovation Management Review*, 7(7), 21–33.

Stephens, E., & Martin, B. (2019). *Business policy and strategic management*. Waltham Abbey Essex: ED - Tech Press.

Stickdorn, M. S., & Schneider, J. (2014). *This is service design thinking: Basics, tools, cases*. Amsterdam: BIS Publishers.

Stilgoe, J., Owen, R., & Macnaghten, P. (2013). Developing a framework for responsible innovation. *Research Policy*, 42(9), 1568–1580. doi: 10.1016/j.respol.2013.05.008

Stoker, G. (2006). Public value management: A new narrative for networked governance? *The American Review of Public Administration*, 36(1), 41–57. doi: 10.1177/0275074005282583

Temmerman, L., Veeckman, C., & Ballon, P. (2021). Collaborative governance platform for social innovation in Brussels. *Social Enterprise Journal*, ahead-of-print. doi: 10.1108/SEJ-12-2019-0101

Toots, M., McBride, K., Kalvet, T., & Krimmer, R. (2017). Open data as enabler of public service co-creation: Exploring the drivers and barriers. In *2017 Conference for E-Democracy and Open Government (CeDEM)* (pp. 102–112). Krems, Austria: IEEE.

Torfing, J., Sørensen, E., & Røiseland, A. (2019). Transforming the public sector into an arena for co-creation: Barriers, drivers, benefits, and ways forward. *Administration & Society*, 51(5), 795–825. doi: 10.1177/0095399716680057

Townsend, A. M. (2013). *Smart cities: Big data, civic hackers, and the quest for a new Utopia*. New York, NY: WW Norton & Company.

Tribe, K. (2019). *Weber, M: Economy and society: A new translation*. Cambridge, MA: Harvard University Press.

Tummers, L., Voorberg, W., & Bekkers, V. (2015). Ten policy recommendations for co-creation during social innovation. *European Policy Brief*.

Turnhout, E., Van Bommel, S., & Aarts, N. (2010). How participation creates citizens: Participatory governance as performative practice. *Ecology and Society*, 15(4), 26–41.

Tuurnas, S., Stenvall, J., Virtanen, P. J., Pekkola, E., & Kurkela, K. (2019). Towards collaborative development culture in local government organisations. *International Journal of Public Sector Management*, 32(6), 582–599. doi: 10.1108/IJPSM-05-2018-0119

Tweddle, J. C., Robinson, L. D., Pocock, M. J. O., & Roy, H. E. (2012). *Guide to citizen science: Developing, implementing and evaluating citizen science to study biodiversity and the environment in the UK* (p. 29). NERC/Centre for Ecology & Hydrology.

United Nations. (n.d.). SDG 11: Make cities and human settlements inclusive, safe, resilient and sustainable. Retrieved from https://www.unodc.org/unodc/en/sustainable-development-goals/sdg11_-sustainable-cities-and-communities.html. Accessed on June 16, 2021.

van der Graaf, S. (2018a). *ComMODify! Mod development at the crossroads of commerce and community*. Cham: Palgrave Macmillan.

van der Graaf, S. (2018b). In Waze We Trust: Algorithmic governance of the public sphere. *Media and Communication*, 6(4), 153–162.

van der Graaf, S. (2020). The right to the city in the platform age: Child-friendly city and smart city premises in contention. *Information, 11*(6), 285. doi: 10.3390/info11060285

van der Graaf, S., & Ballon, P. (2019). Navigating platform urbanism. *Technological Forecasting and Social Change, 142,* 364–372. doi: 10.1016/j.techfore.2018.07.027

van Dijck, J. (2013). *The culture of connectivity: A critical history of social media.* Oxford: Oxford University Press.

Van Dijck, J., & Nieborg, D. (2009). Wikinomics and its discontents: A critical analysis of Web 2.0 business manifestos. *New Media & Society, 11*(5), 855–874. doi: 10.1177/1461444809105356

Vandenabeele, W. (2007). Toward a public administration theory of public service motivation. *Public Management Review, 9*(4), 545–556. doi: 10.1080/14719030701726697

Vargo, S. L., & Lusch, R. F. (2004). Evolving to a new dominant logic for marketing. *Journal of Marketing, 68*(1), 1–17. doi: 10.1509/jmkg.68.1.1.24036

Vargo, S. L., & Lusch, R. F. (2008). Service-dominant logic: Continuing the evolution. *Journal of the Academy of Marketing Science, 36*(1), 1–10. doi: 10.1007/s11747-007-0069-6

Vargo, S. L., & Lusch, R. F. (2016). Institutions and axioms: An extension and update of service-dominant logic. *Journal of the Academy of Marketing Science, 44*(1), 5–23. doi: 10.1007/s11747-015-0456-3

Veeckman, C., Schuurman, D., Leminen, S., & Westerlund, M. (2013). Linking living lab characteristics and their outcomes: Towards a conceptual framework. *Technology Innovation Management Review, 3*(12), 6–15.

Veeckman, C., & Van Der Graaf, S. (2015). The city as living laboratory: Empowering citizens with the Citadel Toolkit. *Technology Innovation Management Review, 5*(3), 6–17.

Verganti, R. (2008). Design, meanings, and radical innovation: A metamodel and a research agenda. *Journal of Product Innovation Management, 25*(5), 436–456.

Vicini, S., Bellini, S., & Sanna, A. (2012). The city of the future living lab. *Journal of Automation and Smart Technology, X,* 1–4. doi: 10.5875/ausmt.vxix.xx

Victorino, L., Field, J. M., Buell, R. W., Dixon, M. J., Meyer Goldstein, S., ... Zhang, J. J. (2018). Service operations: What have we learned? *Journal of Service Management*, 29(1), 39–54. doi: 10.1108/JOSM-08-2017-0192

von Hippel, E. (2005). *Democratizing innovation | The MIT Press*. Cambridge, MA: MIT Press.

Voorberg, W., Bekkers, V., Timeus, K., Tonurist, P., & Tummers, L. (2017). Changing public service delivery: Learning in co-creation. *Policy and Society*, 36(2), 178–194. doi: 10.1080/14494035.2017.1323711

Voorberg, W., Bekkers, V., & Tummers, L. (2015). A systematic review of co-creation and co-production: Embarking on the social innovation journey. *Public Management Review*, 17(9), 1333–1357. doi: 10.1080/14719037. 2014.930505

Walker, R. M., & Andrews, R. (2015). Local government management and performance: A review of evidence. *Journal of Public Administration Research and Theory*. doi: 10.1093/JOPART/MUT038

Walker, R. M., Avellaneda, C. N., & Berry, F. S. (2011). Exploring the diffusion of innovation among high and low innovative localities. *Public Management Review*, 13(1), 95–125. doi: 10.1080/14719037.2010.501616

Walravens, N. (2016, October 27). *'Should there be an App for that?' Public value creation from 'smart' mobile application initiatives for Brussels and local governments*. Unpublished PhD Thesis. Brussels: Vrije Universiteit Brussel.

Warren, M. E. (2009). Governance-driven democratization. *Critical Policy Studies*, 3(1), 3–13.

Weber, J. M., Kopelman, S., & Messick, D. M. (2004). A conceptual review of decision making in social dilemmas: Applying a logic of appropriateness. *Personality and Social Psychology Review*, 8(3), 281–307. doi: 10.1207/ s15327957pspr0803_4

Weible, C. M., & Sabatier, P. A. (2018). *Theories of the policy process*. Routledge.

Wenger, E. (1998). Communities of practice: Learning as a social system. *Systems Thinker*, 9(5), 2–3.

Wenger, E. (2011). Communities of practice: A brief introduction. Retrieved from https://scholarsbank.uoregon.edu/xmlui/handle/1794/11736. Accessed on August 30, 2021.

Wolf, J., Neil Adger, W., Lorenzoni, I., Abrahamson, V., & Raine, R. (2010). Social capital, individual responses to heat waves and climate change adaptation: An empirical study of two UK Cities. *Global Environmental Change*, *20*(1), 44–52. doi: 10.1016/j.gloenvcha.2009.09.004

Wynen, J., & Verhoest, K. (2015). Do NPM-type reforms lead to a cultural revolution within public sector organizations? *Public Management Review*, *17*(3), 356–379. doi: 10.1080/14719037.2013.841459

Young, I. (2002). *Inclusion and democracy*. Oxford: Oxford University Press.

Yu, T., & Wu, N. Q. (2009). A review of study on the competing values framework. *International Journal of Business and Management*, *4*(7), 37. doi: 10.5539/ijbm.v4n7p37

Zambonelli, F., Salim, F., Loke, S. W., De Meuter, W., & Kanhere, S. (2018). Algorithmic governance in smart cities: The conundrum and the potential of pervasive computing solutions. *IEEE Technology and Society Magazine*, *37*(2), 80–87. doi: 10.1109/MTS.2018.2826080

Zorzetti, M., Vaccaro, M., Moralles, C., Prauchner, B., Signoretti, I., Pereira, E., … Marczak, S. (2020). Maturity models for agile, lean startup, and user-centered design in software engineering: A combined systematic literature mapping. In *ICEIS (2)* (pp. 145–156).

INDEX